TO

______________________

ON

______________________

FROM

______________________

# Kregel's TREASURY OF ILLUSTRATED BIBLE STORIES

MATT LOCKHART
General Editor

KREGEL CHILDREN'S

*Kregel's Treasury of Illustrated Bible Stories*


Published by Kregel Publications, a division of Kregel Inc., 2450 Oak Industrial Dr. NE, Grand Rapids, MI 49505.



General Editor: Matt Lockhart
Project Editor: Sarah De Mey
Project Designer: Sarah Slattery



ISBN 978-0-8254-4646-7

Printed in China
25 26 27 28 29 / 5 4 3

# Contents

## OLD TESTAMENT

## Israel in the Time of the Judges



## A Kingdom United



## Elijah and Elisha: Two Powerful Prophets



## Jonah: A Reluctant Messenger



## A Kingdom Divided



## Exile and Beginning Again



## A Prophet Tells of Jesus Coming

# NEW TESTAMENT

## Before Jesus Was Born



## The Birth and Early Days of Jesus



## The Work of John the Baptist



## Jesus Begins His Work



## The Stories and Teachings of Jesus



## The Miracles of Jesus

## The Last Days of Jesus on Earth



## The First Christians and the Early Church



## Glimpses of the Future

# OLD TESTAMENT

# God Creates Space and Light

## Genesis 1

IN THE BEGINNING GOD created the heavens and the earth. The earth was formless and empty, and darkness covered the deep waters. And the Spirit of God was hovering over the surface of the waters.

Then God said, "Let there be light," and there was light. And God saw that the light was good. Then he separated the light from the darkness. God called the light "day" and the darkness "night."

And evening passed and morning came, marking the first day.

Then God said, "Let there be a space between the waters, to separate the waters of the heavens from the waters of the earth." And that is what happened. God made this space to separate the waters of the earth from the waters of the heavens. God called the space "sky."

And evening passed and morning came, marking the second day.

Genesis 1:1–8 (NLT)

# God Creates Land, Plants, and Stars

## Genesis 1

THEN GOD SAID, "Let the waters beneath the sky flow together into one place, so dry ground may appear." And that is what happened. God called the dry ground "land" and the waters "seas." And God saw that it was good. Then God said, "Let the land sprout with vegetation—every sort of seed-bearing plant, and trees that grow seed-bearing fruit. These seeds will then produce the kinds of plants and trees from which they came." And that is what happened. The land produced vegetation—all sorts of seed-bearing plants, and trees with seed-bearing fruit. Their seeds produced plants and trees of the same kind. And God saw that it was good.

And evening passed and morning came, marking the third day.

Then God said, "Let lights appear in the sky to separate the day from the night. Let them be signs to mark the seasons, days, and years. Let these lights in the sky shine down on the earth." And that is what happened. God made two great lights—the larger one to govern the day, and the smaller one to govern the night. He also made the stars. God set these lights in the sky to light the earth, to govern the day and night, and to separate the light from the darkness. And God saw that it was good.

And evening passed and morning came, marking the fourth day.

Genesis 1:9–19 (NLT)

# God Creates Animals and People

## Genesis 1

THEN GOD SAID, "Let the waters swarm with fish and other life. Let the skies be filled with birds of every kind." So God created great sea creatures and every living thing that scurries and swarms in the water, and every sort of bird—each producing offspring of the same kind. And God saw that it was good. Then God blessed them, saying, "Be fruitful and multiply. Let the fish fill the seas, and let the birds multiply on the earth."

And evening passed and morning came, marking the fifth day.

Then God said, "Let the earth produce every sort of animal, each producing offspring of the same kind—livestock, small animals that scurry along the ground, and wild animals." And that is what happened. God made all sorts of wild animals, livestock, and small animals, each able to produce offspring of the same kind. And God saw that it was good.

Then God said, "Let us make human beings in our image, to be like us. They will reign over the fish in the sea, the birds in the sky, the livestock, all the wild animals on the earth, and the small animals that scurry along the ground."

So God created human beings in his own image.
In the image of God he created them;
male and female he created them.

Then God blessed them and said, "Be fruitful and multiply. Fill the earth and govern it. Reign over the fish in the sea, the birds in the sky, and all the animals that scurry along the ground."

Then God said, "Look! I have given you every seed-bearing plant throughout the earth and all the fruit trees for your food. And I have given every green plant as food for all the wild animals, the birds in the sky, and the small animals that scurry along the ground—everything that has life." And that is what happened.

Then God looked over all he had made, and he saw that it was very good!

And evening passed and morning came, marking the sixth day.

Genesis 1:20–31 (NLT)

# Temptation and Sin

## Genesis 2 and 3

THE LORD GOD placed the man in the Garden of Eden to tend and watch over it. But the LORD God warned him, "You may freely eat the fruit of every tree in the garden—except the tree of the knowledge of good and evil. If you eat its fruit, you are sure to die."

### THE MAN AND WOMAN SIN

THE SERPENT was the shrewdest of all the wild animals the LORD God had made. One day he asked the woman, "Did God really say you must not eat the fruit from any of the trees in the garden?"

"Of course we may eat fruit from the trees in the garden," the woman replied. "It's only the fruit from the tree in the middle of the garden that we are not allowed to eat. God said, 'You must not eat it or even touch it; if you do, you will die.'"

"You won't die!" the serpent replied to the woman. "God knows that your eyes will be opened as soon as you eat it, and you will be like God, knowing both good and evil."

The woman was convinced. She saw that the tree was beautiful and its fruit looked delicious, and she wanted the wisdom it would give her. So she took some of the fruit and ate it. Then she gave some to her husband, who was with her, and he ate it, too. At that moment their eyes were opened, and they suddenly felt shame at their nakedness.

Genesis 2:15–17; 3:1–7 (NLT)

# Adam and Eve Sent Out of the Garden

## Genesis 3

LATE IN THE AFTERNOON a breeze began to blow, and the man and woman heard the LORD God walking in the garden. They were frightened and hid behind some trees.

The LORD called out to the man and asked, "Where are you?"

The man answered, "I was naked, and when I heard you walking through the garden, I was frightened and hid!"

"How did you know you were naked?" God asked. "Did you eat any fruit from that tree in the middle of the garden?"

"It was the woman you put here with me," the man said. "She gave me some of the fruit, and I ate it."

The LORD God then asked the woman, "What have you done?"

"The snake tricked me," she answered. "And I ate some of that fruit."

Then the LORD said to the woman,

> "You will suffer terribly
> when you give birth.
>
> But you will still desire
> your husband,
> and he will rule over you."

The LORD said to the man,

> "You listened to your wife
> and ate fruit from that tree.
>
> And so, the ground
> will be under a curse
> because of what you did.
>
> As long as you live,
> you will have to struggle
> to grow enough food.
> Your food will be plants,
> but the ground
> will produce
> thorns and thistles.
> You will have to sweat
> to earn a living;
> you were made out of soil,
> and you will once again
> turn into soil."

Then the LORD God made clothes out of animal skins for the man and his wife.

The LORD said, "These people now know the difference between right and wrong, just as we do. But they must not be allowed to eat fruit from the tree that lets them live forever." So the LORD God sent them out of the Garden of Eden, where they would have to work the ground from which the man had been made.

Genesis 3:8–13, 16–19, 21–23 (CEV)

# Animals Come to Noah's Ark

## Genesis 6 and 8

GOD LOOKED AT THE WORLD and saw that it was evil, for the people were all living evil lives.

God said to Noah, "I have decided to put an end to all people. I will destroy them completely, because the world is full of their violent deeds. Build a boat for yourself out of good timber; make rooms in it and cover it with tar inside and out. Make it 450 feet long, 75 feet wide, and 45 feet high. Make a roof for the boat and leave a space of 18 inches between the roof and the sides. Build it with three decks and put a door in the side. I am going to send a flood on the earth to destroy every living being. Everything on the earth will die, but I will make a covenant with you. Go into the boat with your wife, your sons, and their wives. Take into the boat with you a male and a female of every kind of animal and of every kind of bird, in order to keep them alive. Take along all kinds of food for you and for them."

### THE END OF THE FLOOD

GOD HAD NOT FORGOTTEN Noah and all the animals with him in the boat; he caused a wind to blow, and the water started going down. The outlets of the water beneath the earth and the floodgates of the sky were closed. The rain stopped, and the water gradually went down for 150 days. On the seventeenth day of the seventh month the boat came to rest on a mountain in the Ararat range.

Genesis 6:12–21; 8:1–4 (GNT)

# The Ark and the Dove

## Genesis 8

AFTER ANOTHER FORTY DAYS, Noah opened the window he had made in the boat and released a raven. The bird flew back and forth until the floodwaters on the earth had dried up. He also released a dove to see if the water had receded and it could find dry ground. But the dove could find no place to land because the water still covered the ground. So it returned to the boat, and Noah held out his hand and drew the dove back inside. After waiting another seven days, Noah released the dove again. This time the dove returned to him in the evening with a fresh olive leaf in its beak. Then Noah knew that the floodwaters were almost gone. He waited another seven days and then released the dove again. This time it did not come back.

Genesis 8:6–12 (NLT)

# God's Rainbow of Promise

## Genesis 9

GOD TOLD NOAH and his sons, "I hereby confirm my covenant with you and your descendants, and with all the animals that were on the boat with you—the birds, the livestock, and all the wild animals—every living creature on earth. Yes, I am confirming my covenant with you. Never again will floodwaters kill all living creatures; never again will a flood destroy the earth."

Then God said, "I am giving you a sign of my covenant with you and with all living creatures, for all generations to come. I have placed my rainbow in the clouds. It is the sign of my covenant with you and with all the earth. When I send clouds over the earth, the rainbow will appear in the clouds, and I will remember my covenant with you and with all living creatures. Never again will the floodwaters destroy all life. When I see the rainbow in the clouds, I will remember the eternal covenant between God and every living creature on earth." Then God said to Noah, "Yes, this rainbow is the sign of the covenant I am confirming with all the creatures on earth."

Genesis 9:8–17 (NLT)

E. FAY

# Tower of Babel

## Genesis 11

AT ONE TIME all the people of the world spoke the same language and used the same words. As the people migrated to the east, they found a plain in the land of Babylonia and settled there.

They began saying to each other, "Let's make bricks and harden them with fire." (In this region bricks were used instead of stone, and tar was used for mortar.) Then they said, "Come, let's build a great city for ourselves with a tower that reaches into the sky. This will make us famous and keep us from being scattered all over the world."

But the LORD came down to look at the city and the tower the people were building. "Look!" he said. "The people are united, and they all speak the same language. After this, nothing they set out to do will be impossible for them! Come, let's go down and confuse the people with different languages. Then they won't be able to understand each other."

In that way, the LORD scattered them all over the world, and they stopped building the city. That is why the city was called Babel, because that is where the LORD confused the people with different languages. In this way he scattered them all over the world.

Genesis 11:1–9 (NLT)

# God Calls Abram to a New Land

## Genesis 12

THE LORD HAD SAID to Abram, "Leave your native country, your relatives, and your father's family, and go to the land that I will show you. I will make you into a great nation. I will bless you and make you famous, and you will be a blessing to others. I will bless those who bless you and curse those who treat you with contempt. All the families on earth will be blessed through you."

So Abram departed as the LORD had instructed, and Lot went with him. Abram was seventy-five years old when he left Haran. He took his wife, Sarai, his nephew Lot, and all his wealth—his livestock and all the people he had taken into his household at Haran—and headed for the land of Canaan. When they arrived in Canaan, Abram traveled through the land as far as Shechem. There he set up camp beside the oak of Moreh. At that time, the area was inhabited by Canaanites.

Then the LORD appeared to Abram and said, "I will give this land to your descendants." And Abram built an altar there and dedicated it to the LORD, who had appeared to him. After that, Abram traveled south and set up camp in the hill country, with Bethel to the west and Ai to the east. There he built another altar and dedicated it to the LORD, and he worshiped the LORD. Then Abram continued traveling south by stages toward the Negev.

Genesis 12:1–9 (NLT)

# Abram and Lot Separate

## Genesis 13

ABRAM WAS A VERY RICH MAN, with sheep, goats, and cattle, as well as silver and gold.

Lot also had sheep, goats, and cattle, as well as his own family and servants. And so there was not enough pasture land for the two of them to stay together, because they had too many animals. So quarrels broke out between the men who took care of Abram's animals and those who took care of Lot's animals. (At that time the Canaanites and the Perizzites were still living in the land.)

Then Abram said to Lot, "We are relatives, and your men and my men shouldn't be quarreling. So let's separate. Choose any part of the land you want. You go one way, and I'll go the other."

Lot looked around and saw that the whole Jordan Valley, all the way to Zoar, had plenty of water, like the Garden of the LORD or like the land of Egypt. (This was before the LORD had destroyed the cities of Sodom and Gomorrah.) So Lot chose the whole Jordan Valley for himself and moved away toward the east. That is how the two men parted. Abram stayed in the land of Canaan, and Lot settled among the cities in the valley and camped near Sodom, whose people were wicked and sinned against the LORD.

After Lot had left, the LORD said to Abram, "From where you are, look carefully in all directions. I am going to give you and your descendants all the land that you see, and it will be yours forever. I am going to give you so many descendants that no one will be able to count them all; it would be as easy to count all the specks of dust on earth! Now, go and look over the whole land, because I am going to give it all to you."

Genesis 13:2, 5–17 (GNT)

# Abram Rescues Lot
## Genesis 14

ABOUT THIS TIME WAR BROKE OUT IN THE REGION.

The victorious invaders then plundered Sodom and Gomorrah and headed for home, taking with them all the spoils of war and the food supplies. They also captured Lot—Abram's nephew who lived in Sodom—and carried off everything he owned.

But one of Lot's men escaped and reported everything to Abram the Hebrew, who was living near the oak grove belonging to Mamre the Amorite. Mamre and his relatives, Eshcol and Aner, were Abram's allies.

When Abram heard that his nephew Lot had been captured, he mobilized the 318 trained men who had been born into his household. Then he pursued Kedorlaomer's army until he caught up with them at Dan. There he divided his men and attacked during the night. Kedorlaomer's army fled, but Abram chased them as far as Hobah, north of Damascus. Abram recovered all the goods that had been taken, and he brought back his nephew Lot with his possessions and all the women and other captives.

Genesis 14:1, 11–16 (NLT)

# God's Promise to Abram
## Genesis 15 and 17

THE LORD SPOKE TO ABRAM IN A VISION and said to him, "Do not be afraid, Abram, for I will protect you, and your reward will be great."

But Abram replied, "O Sovereign LORD, what good are all your blessings when I don't even have a son? Since you've given me no children, Eliezer of Damascus, a servant in my household, will inherit all my wealth."

Then the LORD said to him, "No, your servant will not be your heir, for you will have a son of your own who will be your heir." Then the LORD took Abram outside and said to him, "Look up into the sky and count the stars if you can. That's how many descendants you will have!"

And Abram believed the LORD, and the LORD counted him as righteous because of his faith.

Then the LORD told him, "I am the LORD who brought you out of Ur of the Chaldeans to give you this land as your possession."

But Abram replied, "O Sovereign LORD, how can I be sure that I will actually possess it?"

The LORD told him, "Bring me a three-year-old heifer, a three-year-old female goat, a three-year-old ram, a turtledove, and a young pigeon." So Abram presented all these to him and killed them. Then he cut each animal down the middle and laid the halves side by side; he did not, however, cut the birds in half. Some vultures swooped down to eat the carcasses, but Abram chased them away.

After the sun went down and darkness fell, Abram saw a smoking firepot and a flaming torch pass between the halves of the carcasses. So the LORD made a covenant with Abram that day and said, "I have given this land to your descendants, all the way from the border of Egypt to the great Euphrates River."

"What's more, I am changing your name. It will no longer be Abram. Instead, you will be called Abraham, for you will be the father of many nations."

Then God said to Abraham, "Regarding Sarai, your wife—her name will no longer be Sarai. From now on her name will be Sarah."

Genesis 15:1–2, 4–11, 17–18; 17:5, 15 (NLT)

# Three Visitors

## Genesis 18 and 21

ONE HOT SUMMER AFTERNOON Abraham was sitting by the entrance to his tent near the sacred trees of Mamre, when the LORD appeared to him. Abraham looked up and saw three men standing nearby. He quickly ran to meet them, bowed with his face to the ground, and said, "Please come to my home where I can serve you."

Abraham quickly went to his tent and said to Sarah, "Hurry! Get a large sack of flour and make some bread." After saying this, he rushed off to his herd of cattle and picked out one of the best calves, which his servant quickly prepared. He then served his guests some yogurt and milk together with the meat.

While they were eating, he stood near them under the trees, and they asked, "Where is your wife Sarah?"

"She is right there in the tent," Abraham answered.

One of the guests was the LORD, and he said, "I'll come back about this time next year, and when I do, Sarah will already have a son."

Sarah was behind Abraham, listening at the entrance to the tent. Abraham and Sarah were very old, and Sarah was well past the age for having children. So she laughed and said to herself, "Now that I am worn out and my husband is old, will I really know such happiness?"

The LORD asked Abraham, "Why did Sarah laugh? Does she doubt that she can have a child in her old age? I am the LORD! There is nothing too difficult for me. I'll come back next year at the time I promised, and Sarah will already have a son."

Although Abraham was very old, Sarah had a son exactly at the time God had said. Abraham named his son Isaac.

Abraham was a hundred years old when Isaac was born, and Sarah said, "God has made me laugh. Now everyone will laugh with me."

Genesis 18:1–3, 6–14; 21:2–3, 5–6 (CEV)

# A Wife for Isaac
## Genesis 24

ONE DAY, ABRAHAM CALLED in his most trusted servant and said to him, "Solemnly promise me in the name of the LORD, who rules heaven and earth, that you won't choose a wife for my son Isaac from the people here in the land of Canaan. Instead, go back to the land where I was born and find a wife for him from among my relatives."

Soon after that, the servant loaded ten of Abraham's camels with valuable gifts. Then he set out for the city in northern Syria, where Abraham's brother Nahor lived.

When he got there, he let the camels rest near the well outside the city. It was late afternoon, the time when the women came out for water. The servant prayed:

> You, LORD, are the God my master Abraham worships. Please keep your promise to him and let me find a wife for Isaac today. The young women of the city will soon come to this well for water, and I'll ask one of them for a drink. If she gives me a drink and then offers to get some water for my camels, I'll know she is the one you have chosen and that you have kept your promise to my master.

While he was still praying, a beautiful unmarried young woman came by with a water jar on her shoulder. She was Rebekah, the daughter of Bethuel, the son of Abraham's brother Nahor and his wife Milcah. Rebekah walked past Abraham's servant, then went over to the well, and filled her water jar. When she started back, Abraham's servant ran to her and said, "Please let me have a drink of water."

"I'll be glad to," she answered. Then she quickly took the jar from her shoulder and held it while he drank. After he had finished, she said, "Now I'll give your camels all the water they want."

Genesis 24:2–4, 10–19 (CEV)

# Isaac and Rebekah Meet
## Genesis 24

EARLY THE NEXT MORNING, Abraham's servant said, "Send me back to my master."

"But we want Rebekah to stay with us at least ten days," her brother and mother said. "Then she can go."

So they said good-bye to Rebekah and sent her away with Abraham's servant and his men. The woman who had been Rebekah's childhood nurse went along with her. They gave her this blessing as she parted:

> "Our sister, may you become
> the mother of many millions!
> May your descendants be strong
> and conquer the cities of their enemies."

Then Rebekah and her servant girls mounted the camels and followed the man. So Abraham's servant took Rebekah and went on his way.

Meanwhile, Isaac, whose home was in the Negev, had returned from Beer-lahai-roi. One evening as he was walking and meditating in the fields, he looked up and saw the camels coming. When Rebekah looked up and saw Isaac, she quickly dismounted from her camel. "Who is that man walking through the fields to meet us?" she asked the servant.

And he replied, "It is my master." So Rebekah covered her face with her veil. Then the servant told Isaac everything he had done.

And Isaac brought Rebekah into his mother Sarah's tent, and she became his wife. He loved her deeply, and she was a special comfort to him after the death of his mother.

Genesis 24:54–55, 59–67 (NLT)

# Esau's Foolish Trade
## Genesis 25

THE LORD ANSWERED ISAAC'S PRAYER, and Rebekah became pregnant with twins.

As the boys grew up, Esau became a skillful hunter. He was an outdoorsman, but Jacob had a quiet temperament, preferring to stay at home. Isaac loved Esau because he enjoyed eating the wild game Esau brought home, but Rebekah loved Jacob.

One day when Jacob was cooking some stew, Esau arrived home from the wilderness exhausted and hungry. Esau said to Jacob, "I'm starved! Give me some of that red stew!" (This is how Esau got his other name, Edom, which means "red.")

"All right," Jacob replied, "but trade me your rights as the firstborn son."

"Look, I'm dying of starvation!" said Esau. "What good is my birthright to me now?"

But Jacob said, "First you must swear that your birthright is mine." So Esau swore an oath, thereby selling all his rights as the firstborn to his brother, Jacob.

Then Jacob gave Esau some bread and lentil stew. Esau ate the meal, then got up and left. He showed contempt for his rights as the firstborn.

Genesis 25:21, 27–34 (NLT)

# Jacob Lies to His Father

## Genesis 27

ISAAC WAS NOW OLD, and had become blind. He called to his older son Esau, saying, "My son." And Esau answered, "Here I am." Isaac said, "Take your bow and arrows, and go out to the field to get meat for me. Get some food ready for me that I love. Bring it to me to eat, so that before I die I will pray that good will come to you."

Rebekah said to her son Jacob, "I heard your father talking to your brother Esau. He said, 'Bring me some meat. Make good-tasting food for me to eat. And before I die I will pray to the Lord for good to come to you.' So now, my son, listen to what I tell you to do. Go to the flock and bring me two fat young goats. I will cook them into good-tasting food, just what your father loves to eat. Then you will take it to your father for him to eat. So before he dies he will pray for good to come to you."

Then Rebekah took the best clothes that belonged to her older son Esau, that were with her in the house. And she put them on her younger son Jacob. She put the skins of the young goats on his hands and on the smooth part of his neck. And she gave her son Jacob the bread and the good-tasting food she had made.

Then he went to his father and said, "My father." Isaac said, "Here I am. Who are you, my son?" Jacob said to his father, "I am Esau, your first-born. I have done as you told me. Sit up and eat the meat I brought, so you will pray that good will come to me."

When Isaac had finished praying that good would come to Jacob, Jacob left his father Isaac. Just then his brother Esau came in from hunting.

His father Isaac said to him, "Who are you?" He answered, "I am your son, your first-born, Esau." Then Isaac shook all over, and he said, "Who was it then who killed an animal and brought meat to me? I ate all of it before you came! And I prayed that good would come to him! Yes, and good will come to him!"

Esau hated Jacob because his father had prayed that good would come to Jacob.

Genesis 27:1–4, 6–10, 15–19, 30, 32–33, 41 (NLV)

# Jacob Runs Away

## Genesis 28

JACOB LEFT THE TOWN OF BEERSHEBA and started out for Haran. At sunset he stopped for the night and went to sleep, resting his head on a large rock. In a dream he saw a ladder that reached from earth to heaven, and God's angels were going up and down on it.

The LORD was standing beside the ladder and said:

> I am the LORD God who was worshiped by Abraham and Isaac. I will give to you and your family the land on which you are now sleeping. Your descendants will spread over the earth in all directions and will become as numerous as the specks of dust. Your family will be a blessing to all people. Wherever you go, I will watch over you, then later I will bring you back to this land. I won't leave you—I will do all I have promised.

Jacob woke up suddenly and thought, "The LORD is in this place, and I didn't even know it."

When Jacob got up early the next morning, he took the rock that he had used for a pillow and stood it up for a place of worship. Then he poured olive oil on the rock to dedicate it to God, and he named the place Bethel. Before that it had been named Luz.

Jacob solemnly promised God, "If you go with me and watch over me as I travel, and if you give me food and clothes and bring me safely home again, you will be my God."

Genesis 28:10–16, 18–21 (CEV)

# Jacob Travels Back Home

## Genesis 31 and 33

JACOB HEARD THE WORDS of Laban's sons, saying, "Jacob has taken away all that our father had. He has become rich with what had belonged to our father." Jacob saw that Laban did not show him as much favor as he did before. Then the Lord said to Jacob, "Return to the land of your fathers and to those of your family. And I will be with you."

Then Jacob got up and put his children and his wives on camels. He took away all his animals, all the riches he had gathered and all the cattle he had gathered in Paddan-aram. And he left to go to his father Isaac in the land of Canaan.

### JACOB MEETS ESAU

Then Jacob looked up and saw Esau coming with 400 men. So he divided the children among Leah and Rachel and the two women who served him. He put the women who served him and their children in front, and Leah and her children behind them, and Rachel and Joseph behind them. Then Jacob went before them. He bowed to the ground seven times, until he came near his brother. But Esau ran to meet him and put his arms around him and kissed him. And they cried.

Genesis 31:1–3, 17–18; 33:1–4 (NLV)

# Joseph's Colorful Coat
## Genesis 37

JACOB LIVED IN THE LAND where his father had lived as a stranger, in the land of Canaan. This is the story of the children of Jacob and of their children.

When Joseph was seventeen years old, he was caring for the flock with his brothers. The boy was with the sons of Bilhah and Zilpah, his father's wives. And Joseph told his father about how bad they were. Now Israel loved Joseph more than all his sons, because Joseph was born when he was an old man. And Israel made him a long coat of many colors. His brothers saw that their father loved him more than all his brothers. So they hated Joseph and could not speak a kind word to him.

Genesis 37:1–4 (NLV)

# Joseph's Dream
## Genesis 37

ONE NIGHT JOSEPH HAD A DREAM, and when he told his brothers about it, they hated him more than ever. "Listen to this dream," he said. "We were out in the field, tying up bundles of grain. Suddenly my bundle stood up, and your bundles all gathered around and bowed low before mine!"

His brothers responded, "So you think you will be our king, do you? Do you actually think you will reign over us?" And they hated him all the more because of his dreams and the way he talked about them.

Soon Joseph had another dream, and again he told his brothers about it. "Listen, I have had another dream," he said. "The sun, moon, and eleven stars bowed low before me!"

This time he told the dream to his father as well as to his brothers, but his father scolded him. "What kind of dream is that?" he asked. "Will your mother and I and your brothers actually come and bow to the ground before you?" But while his brothers were jealous of Joseph, his father wondered what the dreams meant.

Genesis 37:5–11 (NLT)

# Joseph Sold by His Brothers

## Genesis 37

JOSEPH LEFT AND FOUND HIS BROTHERS in Dothan. But before he got there, they saw him coming and made plans to kill him. They said to one another, "Look, here comes the hero of those dreams! Let's kill him and throw him into a pit and say that some wild animal ate him. Then we'll see what happens to those dreams."

Reuben heard this and tried to protect Joseph from them. "Let's not kill him," he said. "Don't murder him or even harm him. Just throw him into a dry well out here in the desert." Reuben planned to rescue Joseph later and take him back to his father.

When Joseph came to his brothers, they pulled off his fancy coat and threw him into a dry well.

As Joseph's brothers sat down to eat, they looked up and saw a caravan of Ishmaelites coming from Gilead. Their camels were loaded with all kinds of spices that they were taking to Egypt. So Judah said, "What will we gain if we kill our brother and hide his body? Let's sell him to the Ishmaelites and not harm him. After all, he is our brother." And the others agreed.

When the Midianite merchants came by, Joseph's brothers took him out of the well, and for twenty pieces of silver they sold him to the Ishmaelites who took him to Egypt.

Genesis 37:17–28 (CEV)

# Joseph's Brothers Trick Jacob

## Genesis 37

THEN THE BROTHERS KILLED A YOUNG GOAT and dipped Joseph's robe in its blood. They sent the beautiful robe to their father with this message: "Look at what we found. Doesn't this robe belong to your son?"

Their father recognized it immediately. "Yes," he said, "it is my son's robe. A wild animal must have eaten him. Joseph has clearly been torn to pieces!" Then Jacob tore his clothes and dressed himself in burlap. He mourned deeply for his son for a long time. His family all tried to comfort him, but he refused to be comforted. "I will go to my grave mourning for my son," he would say, and then he would weep.

Meanwhile, the Midianite traders arrived in Egypt, where they sold Joseph to Potiphar, an officer of Pharaoh, the king of Egypt. Potiphar was captain of the palace guard.

Genesis 37:31–36 (NLT)

# Joseph in Charge of Potiphar's House

## Genesis 39

THE LORD WAS WITH JOSEPH and made him successful. He lived in the house of his Egyptian master, who saw that the LORD was with Joseph and had made him successful in everything he did. Potiphar was pleased with him and made him his personal servant; so he put him in charge of his house and everything he owned.

Joseph was well-built and good-looking, and after a while his master's wife began to desire Joseph and asked him to go to bed with her. He refused and said to her, "Look, my master does not have to concern himself with anything in the house, because I am here. He has put me in charge of everything he has."

But one day when Joseph went into the house to do his work, none of the house servants was there. She caught him by his robe and said, "Come to bed with me." But he escaped and ran outside, leaving his robe in her hand.

She kept his robe with her until Joseph's master came home. Then she told him: "That Hebrew slave that you brought here came into my room and insulted me. But when I screamed, he ran outside, leaving his robe beside me."

Joseph's master was furious and had Joseph arrested and put in the prison where the king's prisoners were kept, and there he stayed.

Genesis 39:2–4, 6–8, 11–12, 16–20 (GNT)

O.A. Stemler

# Joseph in Prison

## Genesis 39 and 40

THE LORD WAS WITH JOSEPH in the prison and showed him his faithful love. And the LORD made Joseph a favorite with the prison warden. Before long, the warden put Joseph in charge of all the other prisoners and over everything that happened in the prison. The warden had no more worries, because Joseph took care of everything. The LORD was with him and caused everything he did to succeed.

Some time later, Pharaoh's chief cup-bearer and chief baker offended their royal master. Pharaoh became angry with these two officials, and he put them in the prison where Joseph was, in the palace of the captain of the guard. They remained in prison for quite some time, and the captain of the guard assigned them to Joseph, who looked after them.

While they were in prison, Pharaoh's cup-bearer and baker each had a dream one night, and each dream had its own meaning. When Joseph saw them the next morning, he noticed that they both looked upset. "Why do you look so worried today?" he asked them.

And they replied, "We both had dreams last night, but no one can tell us what they mean."

"Interpreting dreams is God's business," Joseph replied. "Go ahead and tell me your dreams."

Genesis 39:21–23; 40:1–8 (NLT)

# Joseph Interprets Pharaoh's Dream

## Genesis 41

AFTER TWO YEARS HAD PASSED, the king of Egypt dreamed that he was standing by the Nile River, when seven cows, fat and sleek, came up out of the river and began to feed on the grass. Then seven other cows came up; they were thin and bony. They came and stood by the other cows on the riverbank, and the thin cows ate up the fat cows. Then the king woke up. He fell asleep again and had another dream. Seven heads of grain, full and ripe, were growing on one stalk. Then seven other heads of grain sprouted, thin and scorched by the desert wind, and the thin heads of grain swallowed the full ones. The king woke up and realized that he had been dreaming. In the morning he was worried, so he sent for all the magicians and wise men of Egypt. He told them his dreams, but no one could explain them to him.

The king sent for Joseph, and he was immediately brought from the prison. After he had shaved and changed his clothes, he came into the king's presence. The king said to him, "I have had a dream, and no one can explain it. I have been told that you can interpret dreams."

Joseph answered, "I cannot, Your Majesty, but God will give a favorable interpretation."

Joseph said to the king, "The two dreams mean the same thing; God has told you what he is going to do. There will be seven years of great plenty in all the land of Egypt. After that, there will be seven years of famine, and all the good years will be forgotten, because the famine will ruin the country."

Genesis 41:1–8, 14–16, 25, 29–30 (GNT)

O. Šteml

# Joseph Put in Charge by Pharaoh
## Genesis 41

THE KING SENT FOR JOSEPH, who was quickly brought out of jail.

The king said to him, "I had a dream, yet no one can explain what it means. I am told that you can interpret dreams."

"Your Majesty," Joseph answered, "I can't do it myself, but God can give a good meaning to your dreams."

> Your Majesty, both of your dreams mean the same thing, and in them God has shown what he is going to do.
>
> Your Majesty, you should find someone who is wise and will know what to do, so that you can put him in charge of all Egypt. Then appoint some other officials to collect one-fifth of every crop harvested in Egypt during the seven years when there is plenty. Give them the power to collect the grain during those good years and to store it in your cities. It can be stored until it is needed during the seven years when there won't be enough grain in Egypt. This will keep the country from being destroyed because of the lack of food.

The king and his officials liked this plan. So the king said to them, "No one could possibly handle this better than Joseph, since the Spirit of God is with him."

The king told Joseph, "God is the one who has shown you these things. No one else is as wise as you are or knows as much as you do. I'm putting you in charge of my palace, and everybody will have to obey you. No one will be over you except me. You are now governor of all Egypt!"

Then the king took off his royal ring and put it on Joseph's finger. He gave him fine clothes to wear and placed a gold chain around his neck. He also let him ride in the chariot next to his own, and people shouted, "Make way for Joseph!"

Genesis 41:14–16, 25, 33–43 (CEV)

# Joseph's Brothers Go to Egypt

## Genesis 41 and 42

SO WITH SEVERE FAMINE everywhere, Joseph opened up the storehouses and distributed grain to the Egyptians, for the famine was severe throughout the land of Egypt.

When Jacob heard that grain was available in Egypt, he said to his sons, "Why are you standing around looking at one another? I have heard there is grain in Egypt. Go down there, and buy enough grain to keep us alive. Otherwise we'll die."

So Joseph's ten older brothers went down to Egypt to buy grain. But Jacob wouldn't let Joseph's younger brother, Benjamin, go with them, for fear some harm might come to him. So Jacob's sons arrived in Egypt along with others to buy food, for the famine was in Canaan as well.

Since Joseph was governor of all Egypt and in charge of selling grain to all the people, it was to him that his brothers came. When they arrived, they bowed before him with their faces to the ground. Joseph recognized his brothers instantly, but he pretended to be a stranger and spoke harshly to them. "Where are you from?" he demanded.

"From the land of Canaan," they replied. "We have come to buy food."

Although Joseph recognized his brothers, they didn't recognize him.

Genesis 41:56; 42:1–8 (NLT)

# Joseph Surprises His Brothers

## Genesis 45

JOSEPH COULD STAND IT NO LONGER. There were many people in the room, and he said to his attendants, "Out, all of you!" So he was alone with his brothers when he told them who he was. Then he broke down and wept. He wept so loudly the Egyptians could hear him, and word of it quickly carried to Pharaoh's palace.

"I am Joseph!" he said to his brothers. "Is my father still alive?" But his brothers were speechless! They were stunned to realize that Joseph was standing there in front of them. "Please, come closer," he said to them. So they came closer. And he said again, "I am Joseph, your brother, whom you sold into slavery in Egypt. But don't be upset, and don't be angry with yourselves for selling me to this place. It was God who sent me here ahead of you to preserve your lives. This famine that has ravaged the land for two years will last five more years, and there will be neither plowing nor harvesting. God has sent me ahead of you to keep you and your families alive and to preserve many survivors. So it was God who sent me here, not you! And he is the one who made me an adviser to Pharaoh—the manager of his entire palace and the governor of all Egypt.

"Now hurry back to my father and tell him, 'This is what your son Joseph says: God has made me master over all the land of Egypt. So come down to me immediately! You can live in the region of Goshen, where you can be near me with all your children and grandchildren, your flocks and herds, and everything you own. I will take care of you there, for there are still five years of famine ahead of us. Otherwise you, your household, and all your animals will starve.'"

Genesis 45:1–11 (NLT)

# Jacob's Descendants Suffer

## Exodus 1

THESE ARE THE NAMES of the sons of Israel (that is, Jacob) who moved to Egypt with their father, each with his family: Reuben, Simeon, Levi, Judah, Issachar, Zebulun, Benjamin, Dan, Naphtali, Gad, and Asher. In all, Jacob had seventy descendants in Egypt, including Joseph, who was already there.

In time, Joseph and all of his brothers died, ending that entire generation. But their descendants, the Israelites, had many children and grandchildren. In fact, they multiplied so greatly that they became extremely powerful and filled the land.

Eventually, a new king came to power in Egypt who knew nothing about Joseph or what he had done. He said to his people, "Look, the people of Israel now outnumber us and are stronger than we are. We must make a plan to keep them from growing even more. If we don't, and if war breaks out, they will join our enemies and fight against us. Then they will escape from the country."

So the Egyptians made the Israelites their slaves. They appointed brutal slave drivers over them, hoping to wear them down with crushing labor. They forced them to build the cities of Pithom and Rameses as supply centers for the king. But the more the Egyptians oppressed them, the more the Israelites multiplied and spread, and the more alarmed the Egyptians became. So the Egyptians worked the people of Israel without mercy. They made their lives bitter, forcing them to mix mortar and make bricks and do all the work in the fields. They were ruthless in all their demands.

Exodus 1:1–14 (NLT)

# Baby Moses in a Basket

## Exodus 1 and 2

PHARAOH GAVE THIS ORDER to all his people: "Throw every newborn Hebrew boy into the Nile River. But you may let the girls live."

### THE BIRTH OF MOSES

ABOUT THIS TIME, a man and woman from the tribe of Levi got married. The woman became pregnant and gave birth to a son. She saw that he was a special baby and kept him hidden for three months. But when she could no longer hide him, she got a basket made of papyrus reeds and waterproofed it with tar and pitch. She put the baby in the basket and laid it among the reeds along the bank of the Nile River. The baby's sister then stood at a distance, watching to see what would happen to him.

Soon Pharaoh's daughter came down to bathe in the river, and her attendants walked along the riverbank. When the princess saw the basket among the reeds, she sent her maid to get it for her. When the princess opened it, she saw the baby. The little boy was crying, and she felt sorry for him. "This must be one of the Hebrew children," she said.

Then the baby's sister approached the princess. "Should I go and find one of the Hebrew women to nurse the baby for you?" she asked.

"Yes, do!" the princess replied. So the girl went and called the baby's mother.

"Take this baby and nurse him for me," the princess told the baby's mother. "I will pay you for your help." So the woman took her baby home and nursed him.

Later, when the boy was older, his mother brought him back to Pharaoh's daughter, who adopted him as her own son. The princess named him Moses, for she explained, "I lifted him out of the water."

Exodus 1:22; 2:1–10 (NLT)

# Moses Flees Egypt
## Exodus 2

When Moses had grown up, he went out to visit his own people, the Hebrews, and he saw how hard they were forced to work. During his visit, he saw an Egyptian beating one of his fellow Hebrews. After looking in all directions to make sure no one was watching, Moses killed the Egyptian and hid the body in the sand.

The next day, when Moses went out to visit his people again, he saw two Hebrew men fighting. "Why are you beating up your friend?" Moses said to the one who had started the fight.

The man replied, "Who appointed you to be our prince and judge? Are you going to kill me as you killed that Egyptian yesterday?"

Then Moses was afraid, thinking, "Everyone knows what I did." And sure enough, Pharaoh heard what had happened, and he tried to kill Moses. But Moses fled from Pharaoh and went to live in the land of Midian.

When Moses arrived in Midian, he sat down beside a well. Now the priest of Midian had seven daughters who came as usual to draw water and fill the water troughs for their father's flocks. But some other shepherds came and chased them away. So Moses jumped up and rescued the girls from the shepherds. Then he drew water for their flocks.

When the girls returned to Reuel, their father, he asked, "Why are you back so soon today?"

"An Egyptian rescued us from the shepherds," they answered. "And then he drew water for us and watered our flocks."

"Then where is he?" their father asked. "Why did you leave him there? Invite him to come and eat with us."

Moses accepted the invitation, and he settled there with him. In time, Reuel gave Moses his daughter Zipporah to be his wife.

Exodus 2:11–21 (NLT)

# Moses and the Burning Bush

## Exodus 3

ONE DAY MOSES was tending the flock of his father-in-law, the priest of Midian. He led the flock far into the wilderness and came to Sinai, the mountain of God. There the angel of the LORD appeared to him in a blazing fire from the middle of a bush. Moses stared in amazement. Though the bush was engulfed in flames, it didn't burn up. "This is amazing," Moses said to himself. "Why isn't that bush burning up? I must go see it."

When the LORD saw Moses coming to take a closer look, God called to him from the middle of the bush, "Moses! Moses!"

"Here I am!" Moses replied.

"Do not come any closer," the LORD warned. "Take off your sandals, for you are standing on holy ground. I am the God of your father—the God of Abraham, the God of Isaac, and the God of Jacob." When Moses heard this, he covered his face because he was afraid to look at God.

Then the LORD told him, "I have certainly seen the oppression of my people in Egypt. I have heard their cries of distress because of their harsh slave drivers. Yes, I am aware of their suffering.

"Look! The cry of the people of Israel has reached me, and I have seen how harshly the Egyptians abuse them. Now go, for I am sending you to Pharaoh. You must lead my people Israel out of Egypt."

But Moses protested to God, "Who am I to appear before Pharaoh? Who am I to lead the people of Israel out of Egypt?"

God answered, "I will be with you. And this is your sign that I am the one who has sent you: When you have brought the people out of Egypt, you will worship God at this very mountain."

Exodus 3:1–7, 9–12 (NLT)

# Confronting Pharaoh the King

## Exodus 5, 6, and 7

MOSES AND AARON WENT TO THE KING of Egypt and told him, "The LORD God says, 'Let my people go into the desert, so they can honor me with a celebration there.'"

"Who is this LORD and why should I obey him?" the king replied. "I refuse to let you and your people go!"

They answered, "The LORD God of the Hebrews, has appeared to us. Please let us walk three days into the desert where we can offer sacrifices to him. If you don't, he may strike us down with terrible troubles or with war."

The king said, "Moses and Aaron, why are you keeping these people from working? Look how many you are keeping from doing their work. Now everyone get back to work!"

### THE LORD'S PROMISE TO MOSES

The LORD God told Moses:

> Soon you will see what I will do to the king. Because of my mighty power, he will let my people go, and he will even chase them out of his country.
>
> But I will make the king so stubborn that he won't listen to you. He won't listen even when I do many terrible things to him and his nation. Then I will bring a final punishment on Egypt, and the king will let Israel's families and tribes go. When this happens, the Egyptians will know that I am the LORD.

Exodus 5:1–5; 6:1; 7:3–5 (CEV)

# Preparing for the Passover

## Exodus 11 and 12

THEN THE LORD SAID TO MOSES, "I will send only one more punishment on the king of Egypt and his people. After that he will let you leave. In fact, he will drive all of you out of here."

Moses then said to the king, "The LORD says, 'At about midnight I will go through Egypt, and every first-born son in Egypt will die, from the king's son, who is heir to the throne, to the son of the slave woman who grinds grain. The first-born of all the cattle will die also. There will be loud crying all over Egypt, such as there has never been before or ever will be again.'"

### THE PASSOVER

The LORD spoke to Moses and Aaron in Egypt: "This month is to be the first month of the year for you. Give these instructions to the whole community of Israel: On the tenth day of this month each man must choose either a lamb or a young goat for his household. Then, on the evening of the fourteenth day of the month, the whole community of Israel will kill the animals. The people are to take some of the blood and put it on the doorposts and above the doors of the houses in which the animals are to be eaten.

"On that night I will go through the land of Egypt, killing every first-born male, both human and animal, and punishing all the gods of Egypt. I am the LORD. The blood on the doorposts will be a sign to mark the houses in which you live. When I see the blood, I will pass over you and will not harm you when I punish the Egyptians."

Exodus 11:1, 4–6; 12:1–3, 6–7, 12–13 (GNT)

# Israel Led by God

## Exodus 12 and 13

PHARAOH SENT FOR MOSES and Aaron during the night. "Get out!" he ordered. "Leave my people—and take the rest of the Israelites with you! Go and worship the LORD as you have requested. Take your flocks and herds, as you said, and be gone. Go, but bless me as you leave." All the Egyptians urged the people of Israel to get out of the land as quickly as possible, for they thought, "We will all die!"

The people of Israel had lived in Egypt for 430 years. In fact, it was on the last day of the 430th year that all the LORD's forces left the land.

### ISRAEL'S WILDERNESS DETOUR

When Pharaoh finally let the people go, God did not lead them along the main road that runs through Philistine territory, even though that was the shortest route to the Promised Land. God said, "If the people are faced with a battle, they might change their minds and return to Egypt." So God led them in a roundabout way through the wilderness toward the Red Sea. Thus the Israelites left Egypt like an army ready for battle.

Moses took the bones of Joseph with him, for Joseph had made the sons of Israel swear to do this. He said, "God will certainly come to help you. When he does, you must take my bones with you from this place."

The Israelites left Succoth and camped at Etham on the edge of the wilderness. The LORD went ahead of them. He guided them during the day with a pillar of cloud, and he provided light at night with a pillar of fire. This allowed them to travel by day or by night. And the LORD did not remove the pillar of cloud or pillar of fire from its place in front of the people.

Exodus 12:31–33, 40–41; 13:17–22 (NLT)

# Crossing the Red Sea
## Exodus 14

WHEN WORD REACHED THE KING of Egypt that the Israelites had fled, Pharaoh and his officials changed their minds. "What have we done, letting all those Israelite slaves get away?" they asked. So Pharaoh harnessed his chariot and called up his troops. He took with him 600 of Egypt's best chariots, along with the rest of the chariots of Egypt, each with its commander.

As Pharaoh approached, the people of Israel looked up and panicked when they saw the Egyptians overtaking them. They cried out to the LORD, and they said to Moses, "Why did you bring us out here to die in the wilderness? Weren't there enough graves for us in Egypt? What have you done to us? Why did you make us leave Egypt? Didn't we tell you this would happen while we were still in Egypt? We said, 'Leave us alone! Let us be slaves to the Egyptians. It's better to be a slave in Egypt than a corpse in the wilderness!'"

But Moses told the people, "Don't be afraid. Just stand still and watch the LORD rescue you today. The Egyptians you see today will never be seen again. The LORD himself will fight for you. Just stay calm."

Then the LORD said to Moses, "Why are you crying out to me? Tell the people to get moving! Pick up your staff and raise your hand over the sea. Divide the water so the Israelites can walk through the middle of the sea on dry ground."

Then Moses raised his hand over the sea, and the LORD opened up a path through the water with a strong east wind. The wind blew all that night, turning the seabed into dry land. So the people of Israel walked through the middle of the sea on dry ground, with walls of water on each side!

Exodus 14:5–7, 10–16, 21–22 (NLT)

# The Songs of Moses and Miriam
## Exodus 15

MOSES AND THE ISRAELITES sang this song in praise of the LORD:

I sing praises to the LORD
for his great victory!

He has thrown the horses
and their riders
into the sea.

The LORD is my strength,
the reason for my song,
because he has saved me.

I praise and honor the LORD—
he is my God
and the God
of my ancestors.
The LORD is his name,
and he is a warrior!

### THE SONG OF MIRIAM

THE LORD covered the royal Egyptian cavalry and chariots with the sea, after the Israelites had walked safely through on dry ground. Miriam the sister of Aaron was a prophet. So she took her tambourine and led the other women out to play their tambourines and to dance. Then she sang to them:

"Sing praises to the LORD
for his great victory!

He has thrown the horses
and their riders into the sea."

Exodus 15:1–3, 19–21 (CEV)

# God Provides Manna

## Exodus 16

ON THE FIFTEENTH DAY of the second month after the Israelites had escaped from Egypt, they left Elim and started through the western edge of the Sinai Desert in the direction of Mount Sinai. There in the desert they started complaining to Moses and Aaron, "We wish the LORD had killed us in Egypt. When we lived there, we could at least sit down and eat all the bread and meat we wanted. But you have brought us out here into this desert, where we are going to starve."

The LORD said to Moses, "I will send bread down from heaven like rain. Each day the people can go out and gather only enough for that day. That's how I will see if they obey me. But on the sixth day of each week they must gather and cook twice as much."

Moses and Aaron told the people, "This evening you will know that the LORD was the one who rescued you from Egypt. And in the morning you will see his glorious power, because he has heard your complaints against him. Why should you grumble to us? Who are we?"

That evening a lot of quails came and landed everywhere in the camp, and the next morning dew covered the ground. After the dew had gone, the desert was covered with thin flakes that looked like frost. The people had never seen anything like this, and they started asking each other, "What is it?"

Moses answered, "This is the bread that the LORD has given you to eat. And he orders you to gather about two quarts for each person in your family—that should be more than enough."

Each morning everyone gathered as much as they needed, and in the heat of the day the rest melted.

The Israelites ate manna for forty years, before they came to the border of Canaan that was a settled land.

Exodus 16:1–7, 13–16, 21, 35–36 (CEV)

# God Provides Water

## Exodus 17

AT THE LORD'S COMMAND, the whole community of Israel left the wilderness of [Sinai] and moved from place to place. Eventually they camped at Rephidim, but there was no water there for the people to drink. So once more the people complained against Moses. "Give us water to drink!" they demanded.

"Quiet!" Moses replied. "Why are you complaining against me? And why are you testing the LORD?"

But tormented by thirst, they continued to argue with Moses. "Why did you bring us out of Egypt? Are you trying to kill us, our children, and our livestock with thirst?"

Then Moses cried out to the LORD, "What should I do with these people? They are ready to stone me!"

The LORD said to Moses, "Walk out in front of the people. Take your staff, the one you used when you struck the water of the Nile, and call some of the elders of Israel to join you. I will stand before you on the rock at Mount Sinai. Strike the rock, and water will come gushing out. Then the people will be able to drink." So Moses struck the rock as he was told, and water gushed out as the elders looked on.

Exodus 17:1–6 (NLT)

# Israel Battles the Amalekites
## Exodus 17

WHILE THE PEOPLE OF ISRAEL were still at Rephidim, the warriors of Amalek attacked them. Moses commanded Joshua, "Choose some men to go out and fight the army of Amalek for us. Tomorrow, I will stand at the top of the hill, holding the staff of God in my hand."

So Joshua did what Moses had commanded and fought the army of Amalek. Meanwhile, Moses, Aaron, and Hur climbed to the top of a nearby hill. As long as Moses held up the staff in his hand, the Israelites had the advantage. But whenever he dropped his hand, the Amalekites gained the advantage. Moses' arms soon became so tired he could no longer hold them up. So Aaron and Hur found a stone for him to sit on. Then they stood on each side of Moses, holding up his hands. So his hands held steady until sunset. As a result, Joshua overwhelmed the army of Amalek in battle.

Exodus 17:8–13 (NLT)

# Moses Receives Wise Advice

## Exodus 18

MOSES' FATHER-IN-LAW now came to visit Moses in the wilderness. He brought Moses' wife and two sons with him, and they arrived while Moses and the people were camped near the mountain of God.

The next day, Moses took his seat to hear the people's disputes against each other. They waited before him from morning till evening.

"This is not good!" Moses' father-in-law exclaimed. "You're going to wear yourself out—and the people, too. This job is too heavy a burden for you to handle all by yourself. Now listen to me, and let me give you a word of advice, and may God be with you. You should continue to be the people's representative before God, bringing their disputes to him. Teach them God's decrees, and give them his instructions. Show them how to conduct their lives. But select from all the people some capable, honest men who fear God and hate bribes. Appoint them as leaders over groups of one thousand, one hundred, fifty, and ten. They should always be available to solve the people's common disputes, but have them bring the major cases to you. Let the leaders decide the smaller matters themselves. They will help you carry the load, making the task easier for you. If you follow this advice, and if God commands you to do so, then you will be able to endure the pressures, and all these people will go home in peace."

Moses listened to his father-in-law's advice and followed his suggestions. He chose capable men from all over Israel and appointed them as leaders over the people. He put them in charge of groups of one thousand, one hundred, fifty, and ten. These men were always available to solve the people's common disputes. They brought the major cases to Moses, but they took care of the smaller matters themselves.

Exodus 18:5, 13, 17–26 (NLT)

# The Lord Comes to Mount Sinai
## Exodus 19

MOSES WENT UP THE MOUNTAIN to meet with the LORD God, who told him to say to the people:

> You saw what I did in Egypt, and you know how I brought you here to me, just as a mighty eagle carries its young. Now if you will faithfully obey me, you will be my very own people. The whole world is mine, but you will be my holy nation and serve me as priests.
>
> Moses, that is what you must tell the Israelites.

After Moses went back, he reported to the leaders what the LORD had said, and they promised, "We will do everything the LORD has commanded." So Moses told the LORD about this.

The LORD said to Moses, "I will come to you in a thick cloud and let the people hear me speak to you. Then they will always trust you." Again Moses reported to the people what the LORD had told him.

Once more the LORD spoke to Moses:

> Go back and tell the people that today and tomorrow they must get themselves ready to meet me. They must wash their clothes and be ready by the day after tomorrow, when I will come down to Mount Sinai, where all of them can see me.

On the morning of the third day there was thunder and lightning. A thick cloud covered the mountain, a loud trumpet blast was heard, and everyone in camp trembled with fear. Moses led them out of the camp to meet God, and they stood at the foot of the mountain.

Mount Sinai was covered with smoke because the LORD had come down in a flaming fire. Smoke poured out of the mountain just like a furnace, and the whole mountain shook. The trumpet blew louder and louder. Moses spoke, and God answered him with thunder.

Exodus 19:3–11, 16–19 (CEV)

# The Ten Commandments

## Exodus 24 and Deuteronomy 5

THE LORD SAID TO MOSES, "Come up on the mountain and stay here for a while. I will give you the two flat stones on which I have written the laws that my people must obey."

Do not worship any god except me.

Do not make idols that look like anything in the sky or on earth or in the ocean under the earth. Don't bow down and worship idols. I am the LORD your God, and I demand all your love. If you reject me and worship idols, I will punish your families for three or four generations. But if you love me and obey my laws, I will be kind to your families for thousands of generations.

Do not misuse my name. I am the LORD your God, and I will punish anyone who misuses my name.

Show respect for the Sabbath Day—it belongs to me. You have six days when you can do your work, but the seventh day of the week belongs to me, your God. No one is to work on that day—not you, your children, your oxen or donkeys or any other animal, not even those foreigners who live in your towns. This special day of rest will remind you that I reached out my mighty arm and rescued you from slavery in Egypt.

Respect your father and mother, and you will live a long and successful life in the land I am giving you.

Do not murder.

Be faithful in marriage.

Do not steal.

Do not tell lies about others.

Do not want anything that belongs to someone else.

Exodus 24:12; Deuteronomy 5:7–21 (CEV)

אנכי יהוה
לא יהיה
לא תשא
זכור את
כבד את
לא תרצח
לא תנאף
לא תגנב
לא תענה
לא תחמד
CLEVELAND WOODWARD

# Gift of the Tabernacle
## Exodus 25

THE LORD SAID TO MOSES, "Tell the people of Israel to bring me their sacred offerings. Accept the contributions from all whose hearts are moved to offer them. Here is a list of sacred offerings you may accept from them:

> gold, silver, and bronze;
>
> blue, purple, and scarlet thread;
>
> fine linen and goat hair for cloth;
>
> tanned ram skins and fine goatskin leather;
>
> acacia wood;
>
> olive oil for the lamps;
>
> spices for the anointing oil and the fragrant incense;
>
> onyx stones, and other gemstones to be set in the ephod and the priest's chestpiece.

"Have the people of Israel build me a holy sanctuary so I can live among them. You must build this Tabernacle and its furnishings exactly according to the pattern I will show you."

Exodus 25:1–9 (NLT)

# Israel Disobeys God's Law

## Exodus 20 and 32

"YOU MUST NOT MAKE FOR YOURSELF AN IDOL of any kind or an image of anything in the heavens or on the earth or in the sea."

When the people saw how long it was taking Moses to come back down the mountain, they gathered around Aaron. "Come on," they said, "make us some gods who can lead us. We don't know what happened to this fellow Moses, who brought us here from the land of Egypt."

The LORD told Moses, "Quick! Go down the mountain! Your people whom you brought from the land of Egypt have corrupted themselves. How quickly they have turned away from the way I commanded them to live! They have melted down gold and made a calf, and they have bowed down and sacrificed to it. They are saying, 'These are your gods, O Israel, who brought you out of the land of Egypt.'"

Then Moses turned and went down the mountain. He held in his hands the two stone tablets inscribed with the terms of the covenant. They were inscribed on both sides, front and back. These tablets were God's work; the words on them were written by God himself.

When Joshua heard the boisterous noise of the people shouting below them, he exclaimed to Moses, "It sounds like war in the camp!"

But Moses replied, "No, it's not a shout of victory nor the wailing of defeat. I hear the sound of a celebration."

When they came near the camp, Moses saw the calf and the dancing, and he burned with anger. He threw the stone tablets to the ground, smashing them at the foot of the mountain. He took the calf they had made and burned it.

Exodus 20:4; 32:1, 7–8, 15–20 (NLT)

# The Tent of Meeting

## Exodus 39 and 40

ALL THE WORK ON THE Tent of the LORD's presence was finally completed. The Israelites had done all the work just as the LORD had commanded Moses. Moses examined everything and saw that they had made it all just as the LORD had commanded. So Moses blessed them.

### THE CLOUD OVER THE TENT OF THE LORD'S PRESENCE

Then the cloud covered the Tent [also known as the Tabernacle] and the dazzling light of the LORD's presence filled it. Because of this, Moses could not go into the Tent. The Israelites moved their camp to another place only when the cloud lifted from the Tent. As long as the cloud stayed there, they did not move their camp. During all their wanderings they could see the cloud of the LORD's presence over the Tent during the day and a fire burning above it during the night.

Exodus 39:32, 42–43; 40:34–38 (GNT)

# Twelve Spies Sent into Canaan

## Numbers 13

THE LORD SAID TO MOSES, "Choose a leader from each tribe and send them into Canaan to explore the land I am giving you."

So Moses sent twelve tribal leaders from Israel's camp in the Paran Desert with orders to explore the land of Canaan.

Before Moses sent them into Canaan, he said:

> After you go through the Southern Desert of Canaan, continue north into the hill country and find out what those regions are like. Be sure to remember how many people live there, how strong they are, and if they live in open towns or walled cities. See if the land is good for growing crops and find out what kinds of trees grow there. It's time for grapes to ripen, so try to bring back some of the fruit that grows there.

### THE MEN REPORT BACK TO THE PEOPLE

After exploring the land of Canaan forty days, the twelve men returned to Kadesh in the Paran Desert and told Moses, Aaron, and the people what they had seen. They showed them the fruit and said:

> Look at this fruit! The land we explored is rich with milk and honey. But the people who live there are strong, and their cities are large and walled. We even saw the three Anakim clans. Besides that, the Amalekites live in the Southern Desert; the Hittites, Jebusites, and Amorites are in the hill country; and the Canaanites live along the Mediterranean Sea and the Jordan River.

Caleb calmed down the crowd and said, "Let's go and take the land. I know we can do it!"

But the other men replied, "Those people are much too strong for us." Then they started spreading rumors and saying, "We won't be able to grow anything in that soil. And the people are like giants."

Numbers 13:1–4, 17–20, 25–32 (CEV)

# Cities of Refuge

## Numbers 35

THE LORD SAID TO MOSES, "Give the following instructions to the people of Israel.

"When you cross the Jordan into the land of Canaan, designate cities of refuge to which people can flee if they have killed someone accidentally. These cities will be places of protection from a dead person's relatives who want to avenge the death. The slayer must not be put to death before being tried by the community. Designate six cities of refuge for yourselves, three on the east side of the Jordan River and three on the west in the land of Canaan. These cities are for the protection of Israelites, foreigners living among you, and traveling merchants. Anyone who accidentally kills someone may flee there for safety."

Numbers 35:9–15 (NLT)

# Moses Sees the Promised Land

## Deuteronomy 32 and 34

THE LORD SAID TO MOSES, "Go to Moab, to the mountains east of the river, and climb Mount Nebo, which is across from Jericho. Look out across the land of Canaan, the land I am giving to the people of Israel as their own special possession. Then you will die there on the mountain."

Then Moses went up to Mount Nebo from the plains of Moab and climbed Pisgah Peak, which is across from Jericho. And the LORD showed him the whole land, from Gilead as far as Dan.

Then the LORD said to Moses, "This is the land I promised on oath to Abraham, Isaac, and Jacob when I said, 'I will give it to your descendants.' I have now allowed you to see it with your own eyes, but you will not enter the land."

There has never been another prophet in Israel like Moses, whom the LORD knew face to face. The LORD sent him to perform all the miraculous signs and wonders in the land of Egypt against Pharaoh, and all his servants, and his entire land. With mighty power, Moses performed terrifying acts in the sight of all Israel.

Deuteronomy 32:48–50; 34:1, 4, 10–12 (NLT)

# Joshua Leads Israel
## Deuteronomy 31 and 34

THEN MOSES SPOKE these words to all Israel. He said to them, "I am 120 years old today. I am no longer able to come and go. And the Lord has told me, 'You will not cross this Jordan.' The Lord your God Himself will cross before you. He will destroy these nations in front of you. And you will take their place. Joshua will cross before you also, as the Lord has said."

Then Moses called Joshua and said to him in front of all Israel, "Be strong and have strength of heart. For you will go with this people into the land the Lord has promised to their fathers to give them. And you will bring them in to take it. The Lord is the One Who goes before you. He will be with you. He will be faithful to you and will not leave you alone. Do not be afraid or troubled."

### THE LORD'S LAST WORDS TO MOSES

The Lord said to Moses, "See, the time for you to die is near. Call Joshua, and go to the meeting tent, so I may tell him what to do." So Moses and Joshua went to the meeting tent.

Then the Lord said to Joshua the son of Nun, "Be strong and have strength of heart. For you will bring the people of Israel into the land I promised them. And I will be with you."

Now Joshua the son of Nun was filled with the spirit of wisdom, for Moses had laid his hands on him. So the people of Israel listened to him and did what the Lord had told Moses.

Deuteronomy 31:1–3, 7–8, 14, 23; 34:9 (NLV)

# Rahab and the Spies

## Joshua 2

JOSHUA THE SON OF NUN sent two men from Shittim to go in secret to learn about the land. He said to them, "Go and spy out the land, and Jericho." So they went and came to the house of Rahab, a woman who sold the use of her body, and they stayed there. Then the king of Jericho was told, "See, men of Israel have come here to spy out the land." So the king of Jericho sent word to Rahab, saying, "Bring out the men who have come to you and have gone into your house. For they have come to spy out all the land." But the woman had taken the two men and hidden them. She said, "Yes, the men came to me. But I did not know where they were from."

And she said to the men,

"Now I have shown you kindness. So I beg of you, promise me by the Lord that you will show kindness to those of my father's house. Give me something to show that you will be faithful. Do not kill my father and mother and my brothers and sisters, and all who belong to them. Save us from death." So the men said to her, "Our life for yours! If you do not tell anyone what we are doing, we will be faithful and show you kindness when the Lord gives us the land."

Then she let them down by a rope through the window. She lived in her house that was built on top of the city wall.

Joshua 2:1–4, 9, 12–15 (NLV)

CLEVELAND
WOODWARD

# Israel Enters the Promised Land

## Joshua 3

EARLY THE NEXT MORNING Joshua and all the Israelites left Acacia Grove and arrived at the banks of the Jordan River, where they camped before crossing. Three days later the Israelite officers went through the camp, giving these instructions to the people: "When you see the Levitical priests carrying the Ark of the Covenant of the LORD your God, move out from your positions and follow them. Since you have never traveled this way before, they will guide you. Stay about half a mile behind them, keeping a clear distance between you and the Ark. Make sure you don't come any closer."

Then Joshua told the people, "Purify yourselves, for tomorrow the LORD will do great wonders among you."

In the morning Joshua said to the priests, "Lift up the Ark of the Covenant and lead the people across the river." And so they started out and went ahead of the people.

So the people left their camp to cross the Jordan, and the priests who were carrying the Ark of the Covenant went ahead of them. It was the harvest season, and the Jordan was overflowing its banks. But as soon as the feet of the priests who were carrying the Ark touched the water at the river's edge, the water above that point began backing up a great distance away at a town called Adam, which is near Zarethan. And the water below that point flowed on to the Dead Sea until the riverbed was dry. Then all the people crossed over near the town of Jericho.

Joshua 3:1–6, 14–16 (NLT)

# A Monument of Twelve Stones

## Joshua 4

WHEN ALL THE PEOPLE had crossed the Jordan, the LORD said to Joshua, "Now choose twelve men, one from each tribe. Tell them, 'Take twelve stones from the very place where the priests are standing in the middle of the Jordan. Carry them out and pile them up at the place where you will camp tonight.'"

So Joshua called together the twelve men he had chosen—one from each of the tribes of Israel. He told them, "Go into the middle of the Jordan, in front of the Ark of the LORD your God. Each of you must pick up one stone and carry it out on your shoulder—twelve stones in all, one for each of the twelve tribes of Israel. We will use these stones to build a memorial. In the future your children will ask you, 'What do these stones mean?' Then you can tell them, 'They remind us that the Jordan River stopped flowing when the Ark of the LORD's Covenant went across.' These stones will stand as a memorial among the people of Israel forever."

So the men did as Joshua had commanded them. They took twelve stones from the middle of the Jordan River, one for each tribe, just as the LORD had told Joshua. They carried them to the place where they camped for the night and constructed the memorial there.

Joshua 4:1–8 (NLT)

# The Walls of Jericho Fall

## Joshua 6

NOW THE GATES OF JERICHO were tightly shut because the people were afraid of the Israelites. No one was allowed to go out or in. But the LORD said to Joshua, "I have given you Jericho, its king, and all its strong warriors. You and your fighting men should march around the town once a day for six days. Seven priests will walk ahead of the Ark, each carrying a ram's horn. On the seventh day you are to march around the town seven times, with the priests blowing the horns. When you hear the priests give one long blast on the rams' horns, have all the people shout as loud as they can. Then the walls of the town will collapse, and the people can charge straight into the town."

After Joshua spoke to the people, the seven priests with the rams' horns started marching in the presence of the LORD, blowing the horns as they marched. And the Ark of the LORD's Covenant followed behind them.

On the second day they again marched around the town once and returned to the camp. They followed this pattern for six days.

On the seventh day the Israelites got up at dawn and marched around the town as they had done before. But this time they went around the town seven times. The seventh time around, as the priests sounded the long blast on their horns, Joshua commanded the people, "Shout! For the LORD has given you the town!"

When the people heard the sound of the rams' horns, they shouted as loud as they could. Suddenly, the walls of Jericho collapsed, and the Israelites charged straight into the town and captured it.

Joshua 6:1–5, 8, 14–16, 20 (NLT)

# Joshua at the Battle of Ai

## Joshua 8

THE LORD SAID TO JOSHUA, "Do not be afraid or discouraged. Take all your fighting men and attack Ai, for I have given you the king of Ai, his people, his town, and his land. You will destroy them as you destroyed Jericho and its king. But this time you may keep the plunder and the livestock for yourselves. Set an ambush behind the town."

So Joshua and all the fighting men set out to attack Ai. Joshua chose 30,000 of his best warriors and sent them out at night with these orders: "Hide in ambush close behind the town and be ready for action. When our main army attacks, the men of Ai will come out to fight as they did before, and we will run away from them. We will let them chase us until we have drawn them away from the town. For they will say, 'The Israelites are running away from us as they did before.' Then, while we are running from them, you will jump up from your ambush and take possession of the town, for the LORD your God will give it to you."

Then the LORD said to Joshua, "Point the spear in your hand toward Ai, for I will hand the town over to you." Joshua did as he was commanded. As soon as Joshua gave this signal, all the men in ambush jumped up from their position and poured into the town. They quickly captured it and set it on fire.

Joshua 8:1–7, 18–19 (NLT)

# Joshua and the Witness Stone

## Joshua 24

JOSHUA WARNED THE PEOPLE, "If you abandon the LORD and serve other gods, he will turn against you and destroy you, even though he has been so good to you."

But the people answered Joshua, "No, we will serve the LORD!"

"You are a witness to your own decision," Joshua said. "You have chosen to serve the LORD."

"Yes," they replied, "we are witnesses to what we have said."

"All right then," Joshua said, "destroy the idols among you, and turn your hearts to the LORD, the God of Israel."

The people said to Joshua, "We will serve the LORD our God. We will obey him alone."

So Joshua made a covenant with the people that day at Shechem, committing them to follow the decrees and regulations of the LORD. Joshua recorded these things in the Book of God's Instructions. As a reminder of their agreement, he took a huge stone and rolled it beneath the terebinth tree beside the Tabernacle of the LORD.

Joshua said to all the people, "This stone has heard everything the LORD said to us. It will be a witness to testify against you if you go back on your word to God."

Then Joshua sent all the people away to their own homelands.

After this, Joshua son of Nun, the servant of the LORD, died at the age of 110.

The people of Israel served the LORD throughout the lifetime of Joshua and of the elders who outlived him—those who had personally experienced all that the LORD had done for Israel.

Joshua 24:19–29, 31 (NLT)

# Israel Worships Other Gods

## Judges 2

JOSHUA SON OF NUN, the servant of the LORD, died at the age of 110.

After that generation died, another generation grew up who did not acknowledge the LORD or remember the mighty things he had done for Israel.

The Israelites did evil in the LORD's sight and served the images of Baal. They abandoned the LORD, the God of their ancestors, who had brought them out of Egypt. They went after other gods, worshiping the gods of the people around them. And they angered the LORD. They abandoned the LORD to serve Baal and the images of Ashtoreth. This made the LORD burn with anger against Israel, so he handed them over to raiders who stole their possessions. He turned them over to their enemies all around, and they were no longer able to resist them. Every time Israel went out to battle, the LORD fought against them, causing them to be defeated, just as he had warned. And the people were in great distress.

### THE LORD RESCUES HIS PEOPLE

Then the LORD raised up judges to rescue the Israelites from their attackers. Yet Israel did not listen to the judges but prostituted themselves by worshiping other gods. How quickly they turned away from the path of their ancestors, who had walked in obedience to the LORD's commands.

Whenever the LORD raised up a judge over Israel, he was with that judge and rescued the people from their enemies throughout the judge's lifetime. For the LORD took pity on his people, who were burdened by oppression and suffering. But when the judge died, the people returned to their corrupt ways, behaving worse than those who had lived before them. They went after other gods, serving and worshiping them. And they refused to give up their evil practices and stubborn ways.

Judges 2:8, 10–19 (NLT)

# Deborah Leads Israel

## Judges 4

AFTER EHUD'S DEATH, the Israelites again did evil in the LORD's sight. So the LORD turned them over to King Jabin of Hazor, a Canaanite king. The commander of his army was Sisera, who lived in Harosheth-haggoyim. Sisera, who had 900 iron chariots, ruthlessly oppressed the Israelites for twenty years. Then the people of Israel cried out to the LORD for help.

Deborah, the wife of Lappidoth, was a prophet who was judging Israel at that time. She would sit under the Palm of Deborah, between Ramah and Bethel in the hill country of Ephraim, and the Israelites would go to her for judgment. One day she sent for Barak son of Abinoam, who lived in Kedesh in the land of Naphtali. She said to him, "This is what the LORD, the God of Israel, commands you: Call out 10,000 warriors from the tribes of Naphtali and Zebulun at Mount Tabor. And I will call out Sisera, commander of Jabin's army, along with his chariots and warriors, to the Kishon River. There I will give you victory over him."

Barak told her, "I will go, but only if you go with me."

"Very well," she replied, "I will go with you. But you will receive no honor in this venture, for the LORD's victory over Sisera will be at the hands of a woman." So Deborah went with Barak to Kedesh.

Then Deborah said to Barak, "Get ready! This is the day the LORD will give you victory over Sisera, for the LORD is marching ahead of you." So Barak led his 10,000 warriors down the slopes of Mount Tabor into battle.

Judges 4:1–9, 14 (NLT)

# An Angel Visits Gideon

## Judges 6

THEN THE PEOPLE OF ISRAEL sinned in the eyes of the Lord. And the Lord gave them into the hands of Midian for seven years. Midian was stronger than Israel. Because of Midian the people of Israel made big caves in the sides of the mountains where they could live which were safe places for themselves. For when Israel had planted seeds, the Midianites and Amalekites and the people of the east would come and fight against them.

The people of Israel cried to the Lord because of Midian.

Then the angel of the Lord came and sat under the oak tree in Ophrah, which belonged to Joash the Abiezrite. The angel came as Joash's son Gideon was beating out grain where grapes are crushed, to save it from the Midianites. The angel of the Lord showed himself to Gideon and said to him, "The Lord is with you, O powerful soldier." Gideon said to him, "O sir, if the Lord is with us, why has all this happened to us? Where are all His powerful works which our fathers told us about? They said, 'Did not the Lord bring us out of Egypt?' But now the Lord has left us alone. He has put us under the power of Midian." The Lord looked at him and said, "Go in this strength of yours. And save Israel from the power of Midian. Have I not sent you?" Gideon said to Him, "O Lord, how can I save Israel? See, my family is the least in Manasseh. And I am the youngest in my father's house." But the Lord said to him, "For sure I will be with you. You will destroy Midian as one man."

Judges 6:1–3, 7, 11–16 (NLV)

# Gideon's Army Put to the Test

## Judges 7

JERUB-BAAL (THAT IS, GIDEON) and his army got up early and went as far as the spring of Harod. The armies of Midian were camped north of them in the valley near the hill of Moreh. The LORD said to Gideon, "You have too many warriors with you. If I let all of you fight the Midianites, the Israelites will boast to me that they saved themselves by their own strength. Therefore, tell the people, 'Whoever is timid or afraid may leave this mountain and go home.'" So 22,000 of them went home, leaving only 10,000 who were willing to fight.

But the LORD told Gideon, "There are still too many! Bring them down to the spring, and I will test them to determine who will go with you and who will not." When Gideon took his warriors down to the water, the LORD told him, "Divide the men into two groups. In one group put all those who cup water in their hands and lap it up with their tongues like dogs. In the other group put all those who kneel down and drink with their mouths in the stream." Only 300 of the men drank from their hands. All the others got down on their knees and drank with their mouths in the stream.

The LORD told Gideon, "With these 300 men I will rescue you and give you victory over the Midianites. Send all the others home." So Gideon collected the provisions and rams' horns of the other warriors and sent them home. But he kept the 300 men with him.

The Midianite camp was in the valley just below Gideon.

Judges 7:1–8 (NLT)

# Gideon and the Three Hundred

## Judges 7

THAT NIGHT THE LORD commanded Gideon, "Get up and attack the camp; I am giving you victory over it. But if you are afraid to attack, go down to the camp with your servant Purah. You will hear what they are saying, and then you will have the courage to attack."

When Gideon arrived, he heard a man telling a friend about a dream. He was saying, "I dreamed that a loaf of barley bread rolled into our camp and hit a tent. The tent collapsed and lay flat on the ground."

His friend replied, "It's the sword of the Israelite, Gideon son of Joash! It can't mean anything else! God has given him victory over Midian and our whole army!"

When Gideon heard about the man's dream and what it meant, he fell to his knees and worshiped the LORD. Then he went back to the Israelite camp and said, "Get up! The LORD is giving you victory over the Midianite army!" He divided his three hundred men into three groups and gave each man a trumpet and a jar with a torch inside it. He told them, "When I get to the edge of the camp, watch me, and do what I do. When my group and I blow our trumpets, then you blow yours all around the camp and shout, 'For the LORD and for Gideon!'"

Gideon and his one hundred men came to the edge of the camp a while before midnight, just after the guard had been changed. Then they blew the trumpets and broke the jars they were holding, and the other two groups did the same. They all held the torches in their left hands, the trumpets in their right, and shouted, "A sword for the LORD and for Gideon!"

While Gideon's men were blowing their trumpets, the LORD made the enemy troops attack each other with their swords.

Judges 7:9–11, 13–20, 22 (GNT)

# The Story of Samson

## Judges 13, 15, and 16

IN THOSE DAYS A MAN NAMED MANOAH from the tribe of Dan lived in the town of Zorah.

The angel of the LORD appeared to Manoah's wife and said, "You will soon become pregnant and give birth to a son. So be careful; you must not drink wine or any other alcoholic drink nor eat any forbidden food. And his hair must never be cut. For he will be dedicated to God as a Nazirite from birth. He will begin to rescue Israel from the Philistines."

When her son was born, she named him Samson. And the LORD blessed him as he grew up.

Samson judged Israel for twenty years during the period when the Philistines dominated the land.

So the Philistines captured him and gouged out his eyes. The Philistine rulers held a great festival, offering sacrifices and praising their god, Dagon. They said, "Our god has given us victory over our enemy Samson!"

Half drunk by now, the people demanded, "Bring out Samson so he can amuse us!" So he was brought from the prison to amuse them, and they had him stand between the pillars supporting the roof.

Samson said to the young servant who was leading him by the hand, "Place my hands against the pillars that hold up the temple. I want to rest against them."

Then Samson prayed to the LORD, "Sovereign LORD, remember me again. O God, please strengthen me just one more time. With one blow let me pay back the Philistines for the loss of my two eyes." Then Samson put his hands on the two center pillars that held up the temple. Pushing against them with both hands, he prayed, "Let me die with the Philistines." And the temple crashed down on the Philistine rulers and all the people.

Judges 13:2–5, 24; 15:20; 16:21, 23, 25–26, 28–30 (NLT)

Schnorr

# Ruth Stays with Naomi

## Ruth 1

BEFORE ISRAEL was ruled by kings, Elimelech from the tribe of Ephrath lived in the town of Bethlehem. His wife was named Naomi, and their two sons were Mahlon and Chilion. But when their crops failed, they moved to the country of Moab. And while they were there, Elimelech died, leaving Naomi with only her two sons.

Later, Naomi's sons married Moabite women. One was named Orpah and the other Ruth. About ten years later, Mahlon and Chilion also died. Now Naomi had no husband or sons.

When Naomi heard that the LORD had given his people a good harvest, she and her two daughters-in-law got ready to leave Moab and go to Judah. As they were on their way there, Naomi said to them, "Don't you want to go back home to your own mothers? You were kind to my husband and sons, and you have always been kind to me. I pray that the LORD will be just as kind to you. May he give each of you another husband and a home of your own."

Naomi kissed them. They cried and said, "We want to go with you and live among your people."

But she replied, "My daughters, why don't you return home? What good will it do you to go with me? Do you think I could have more sons for you to marry?"

They cried again. Orpah kissed her mother-in-law good-by, but Ruth held on to her. Naomi then said to Ruth, "Look, your sister-in-law is going back to her people and to her gods! Why don't you go with her?"

Ruth answered,

"Please don't tell me
    to leave you
    and return home!
I will go where you go,
    I will live where you live;
your people will be my people,
    your God will be my God."

When Naomi saw that Ruth had made up her mind to go with her, she stopped urging her to go back.

Ruth 1:1–11, 14–16, 18 (CEV)

CLEVELAND
WOODWARD

# Ruth Gathers Grain in Boaz's Field

## Ruth 2 and 4

ONE DAY, RUTH SAID TO NAOMI, "Let me see if I can find someone who will let me pick up the grain left in the fields by the harvest workers."

Naomi answered, "Go ahead, my daughter." So right away, Ruth went out to pick up grain in a field owned by Boaz. He was a relative of Naomi's husband Elimelech, as well as a rich and important man.

When Boaz left Bethlehem and went out to his field, he said to the harvest workers, "The LORD bless you!"

They replied, "And may the LORD bless you!"

Then Boaz asked the man in charge of the harvest workers, "Who is that young woman?"

The man answered, "She is the one who came back from Moab with Naomi. She asked if she could pick up grain left by the harvest workers, and she has been working all morning without a moment's rest."

Boaz went over to Ruth and said, "I think it would be best for you not to pick up grain in anyone else's field. Stay here with the women and follow along behind them, as they gather up what the men have cut."

Ruth worked in the field until evening. Then after she had pounded the grain off the stalks, she had a large basket full of grain. She took the grain to town and showed Naomi how much she had picked up. Ruth also gave her the food left over from her lunch.

Naomi said, "Where did you work today? Whose field was it? God bless the man who treated you so well!" Then Ruth told her that she had worked in the field of a man named Boaz.

"The LORD bless Boaz!" Naomi replied. "Boaz is a close relative, one of those who is supposed to look after us."

Boaz married Ruth, and the LORD blessed her with a son.

Ruth 2:1–9, 17–20; 4:13 (CEV)

# Hannah Dedicates Samuel

## 1 Samuel 1

ONCE AFTER A SACRIFICIAL MEAL at Shiloh, Hannah got up and went to pray. Eli the priest was sitting at his customary place beside the entrance of the Tabernacle. Hannah was in deep anguish, crying bitterly as she prayed to the LORD. And she made this vow: "O LORD of Heaven's Armies, if you will look upon my sorrow and answer my prayer and give me a son, then I will give him back to you. He will be yours for his entire lifetime, and as a sign that he has been dedicated to the LORD, his hair will never be cut."

As she was praying to the LORD, Eli watched her. Seeing her lips moving but hearing no sound, he thought she had been drinking. "Must you come here drunk?" he demanded. "Throw away your wine!"

"Oh no, sir!" she replied. "I haven't been drinking wine or anything stronger. But I am very discouraged, and I was pouring out my heart to the LORD."

### SAMUEL'S BIRTH AND DEDICATION

The LORD remembered her plea, and in due time she gave birth to a son. She named him Samuel, for she said, "I asked the LORD for him."

When the child was weaned, Hannah took him to the Tabernacle in Shiloh. They brought along a three-year-old bull for the sacrifice and a basket of flour and some wine. After sacrificing the bull, they brought the boy to Eli. "Sir, do you remember me?" Hannah asked. "I am the very woman who stood here several years ago praying to the LORD. I asked the LORD to give me this boy, and he has granted my request. Now I am giving him to the LORD, and he will belong to the LORD his whole life."

1 Samuel 1:9–15, 19–20, 24–28 (NLT)

# God Speaks to Samuel

## 1 Samuel 3

THE BOY SAMUEL served the LORD by assisting Eli. Now in those days messages from the LORD were very rare, and visions were quite uncommon.

One night Eli, who was almost blind by now, had gone to bed. The lamp of God had not yet gone out, and Samuel was sleeping in the Tabernacle near the Ark of God. Suddenly the LORD called out, "Samuel!"

"Yes?" Samuel replied. "What is it?" He got up and ran to Eli. "Here I am. Did you call me?"

"I didn't call you," Eli replied. "Go back to bed." So he did.

Then the LORD called out again, "Samuel!"

Again Samuel got up and went to Eli. "Here I am. Did you call me?"

"I didn't call you, my son," Eli said. "Go back to bed."

Samuel did not yet know the LORD because he had never had a message from the LORD before. So the LORD called a third time, and once more Samuel got up and went to Eli. "Here I am. Did you call me?"

Then Eli realized it was the LORD who was calling the boy. So he said to Samuel, "Go and lie down again, and if someone calls again, say, 'Speak, LORD, your servant is listening.'" So Samuel went back to bed.

And the LORD came and called as before, "Samuel! Samuel!"

And Samuel replied, "Speak, your servant is listening."

Then the LORD said to Samuel, "I am about to do a shocking thing in Israel. I am going to carry out all my threats against Eli and his family, from beginning to end. I have warned him that judgment is coming upon his family forever, because his sons are blaspheming God and he hasn't disciplined them."

As Samuel grew up, the LORD was with him, and everything Samuel said proved to be reliable.

1 Samuel 3:1–13, 19 (NLT)

EMLER.

# Samuel Leads Israel

## 1 Samuel 7

SAMUEL SAID to all the people of Israel, "If you want to return to the LORD with all your hearts, get rid of your foreign gods and your images of Ashtoreth. Turn your hearts to the LORD and obey him alone; then he will rescue you from the Philistines." So the Israelites got rid of their images of Baal and Ashtoreth and worshiped only the LORD.

Then Samuel told them, "Gather all of Israel to Mizpah, and I will pray to the LORD for you."

When the Philistine rulers heard that Israel had gathered at Mizpah, they mobilized their army and advanced. The Israelites were badly frightened when they learned that the Philistines were approaching. "Don't stop pleading with the LORD our God to save us from the Philistines!" they begged Samuel. So Samuel took a young lamb and offered it to the LORD as a whole burnt offering. He pleaded with the LORD to help Israel, and the LORD answered him.

Just as Samuel was sacrificing the burnt offering, the Philistines arrived to attack Israel. But the LORD spoke with a mighty voice of thunder from heaven that day, and the Philistines were thrown into such confusion that the Israelites defeated them.

Samuel then took a large stone and placed it between the towns of Mizpah and Jeshanah. He named it Ebenezer (which means "the stone of help"), for he said, "Up to this point the LORD has helped us!"

So the Philistines were subdued and didn't invade Israel again for some time. And throughout Samuel's lifetime, the LORD's powerful hand was raised against the Philistines.

1 Samuel 7:3–5, 7–10, 12–13 (NLT)

# Israel's First King

## 1 Samuel 8 and 10

AS SAMUEL GREW OLD, he appointed his sons to be judges over Israel.

Finally, all the elders of Israel met at Ramah to discuss the matter with Samuel. "Look," they told him, "you are now old, and your sons are not like you. Give us a king to judge us like all the other nations have."

### SAMUEL ANOINTS SAUL AS KING

THEN SAMUEL TOOK A FLASK of olive oil and poured it over Saul's head. He kissed Saul and said, "I am doing this because the LORD has appointed you to be the ruler over Israel, his special possession."

Later Samuel called all the people of Israel to meet before the LORD at Mizpah. And he said, "This is what the LORD, the God of Israel, has declared: I brought you from Egypt and rescued you from the Egyptians and from all of the nations that were oppressing you. But though I have rescued you from your misery and distress, you have rejected your God today and have said, 'No, we want a king instead!' Now, therefore, present yourselves before the LORD by tribes and clans."

So Samuel brought all the tribes of Israel before the LORD, and the tribe of Benjamin was chosen by lot. Then he brought each family of the tribe of Benjamin before the LORD, and the family of the Matrites was chosen. And finally Saul son of Kish was chosen from among them. But when they looked for him, he had disappeared! So they asked the LORD, "Where is he?"

And the LORD replied, "He is hiding among the baggage." So they found him and brought him out, and he stood head and shoulders above anyone else.

Then Samuel said to all the people, "This is the man the LORD has chosen as your king. No one in all Israel is like him!"

And all the people shouted, "Long live the king!"

1 Samuel 8:1, 4–5; 10:1, 17–24 (NLT)

# Samuel Addresses Israel

## 1 Samuel 12

SAMUEL SAID TO THE PEOPLE of Israel, "I have done what you asked me to do. I have given you a king to rule you, and now you have him to lead you. As for me, I am old and gray, and my sons are with you. I have been your leader from my youth until now. Here I am. If I have done anything wrong, accuse me now in the presence of the LORD and the king he has chosen. Have I taken anybody's cow or anybody's donkey? Have I cheated or oppressed anyone? Have I accepted a bribe from anyone? If I have done any of these things, I will pay back what I have taken."

The people answered, "No, you have not cheated us or oppressed us; you have not taken anything from anyone."

Samuel replied, "The LORD and the king he has chosen are witnesses today that you have found me to be completely innocent."

"Yes, the LORD is our witness," they answered.

"But when you saw that King Nahash of Ammon was about to attack you, you rejected the LORD as your king and said to me, 'We want a king to rule us.'

"Now here is the king you chose; you asked for him, and now the LORD has given him to you. All will go well with you if you honor the LORD your God, serve him, listen to him, and obey his commands, and if you and your king follow him. But if you do not listen to the LORD but disobey his commands, he will be against you and your king."

1 Samuel 12:1–5, 12–15 (GNT)

# Saul Disobeys the Lord

## 1 Samuel 15

ONE DAY, SAMUEL TOLD SAUL:

The LORD had me choose you to be king of his people, Israel. Now listen to this message from the LORD: "When the Israelites were on their way out of Egypt, the nation of Amalek attacked them. I am the LORD All-Powerful, and now I am going to make Amalek pay!

"Go and attack the Amalekites! Destroy them and all their possessions. Slaughter their cattle, sheep, camels, and donkeys."

The LORD told Samuel, "Saul has stopped obeying me, and I'm sorry that I made him king."

Samuel was angry, and he cried out in prayer to the LORD all night. Early the next morning he went to talk with Saul.

Samuel finally caught up with Saul, and Saul told him, "I hope the LORD will bless you! I have done what the LORD told me."

"Then why," Samuel asked, "do I hear sheep and cattle?"

"The army took them from the Amalekites," Saul explained. "They kept the best sheep and cattle, so they could sacrifice them to the LORD your God. But we destroyed everything else."

"Tell me," Samuel said. "Does the LORD really want sacrifices and offerings? No! He doesn't want your sacrifices. He wants you to obey him. Rebelling against God or disobeying him because you are proud is just as bad as worshiping idols or asking them for advice. You refused to do what God told you, so God has decided that you can't be king."

"I have sinned," Saul admitted. "I disobeyed both you and the LORD. Please forgive me and come back with me so I can worship the LORD."

"No!" Samuel replied, "You disobeyed the LORD, and I won't go back with you. Now the LORD has said that you can't be king of Israel any longer."

1 Samuel 15:1–3, 10–15, 22–26 (CEV)

# David Anointed as Future King

## 1 Samuel 16

NOW THE LORD SAID to Samuel, "You have mourned long enough for Saul. I have rejected him as king of Israel, so fill your flask with olive oil and go to Bethlehem. Find a man named Jesse who lives there, for I have selected one of his sons to be my king."

When they arrived, Samuel took one look at Eliab and thought, "Surely this is the LORD's anointed!"

But the LORD said to Samuel, "Don't judge by his appearance or height, for I have rejected him. The LORD doesn't see things the way you see them. People judge by outward appearance, but the LORD looks at the heart."

Then Jesse told his son Abinadab to step forward and walk in front of Samuel. But Samuel said, "This is not the one the LORD has chosen." Next Jesse summoned Shimea, but Samuel said, "Neither is this the one the LORD has chosen." In the same way all seven of Jesse's sons were presented to Samuel. But Samuel said to Jesse, "The LORD has not chosen any of these." Then Samuel asked, "Are these all the sons you have?"

"There is still the youngest," Jesse replied. "But he's out in the fields watching the sheep and goats."

"Send for him at once," Samuel said. "We will not sit down to eat until he arrives."

So Jesse sent for him. He was dark and handsome, with beautiful eyes.

And the LORD said, "This is the one; anoint him."

So as David stood there among his brothers, Samuel took the flask of olive oil he had brought and anointed David with the oil. And the Spirit of the LORD came powerfully upon David from that day on.

1 Samuel 16:1, 6–13 (NLT)

# David the Shepherd Boy

## Psalm 23

THE LORD IS MY SHEPHERD; I shall not want.
He maketh me to lie down in green pastures:
he leadeth me beside the still waters.
He restoreth my soul:
he leadeth me in the paths of righteousness for his name's sake.
Yea, though I walk through the valley of the shadow of death,
I will fear no evil: for thou art with me;
thy rod and thy staff they comfort me.
Thou preparest a table before me in the presence of mine enemies:
thou anointest my head with oil; my cup runneth over.
Surely goodness and mercy shall follow me all the days of my life:
and I will dwell in the house of the LORD for ever.

Psalm 23:1–6 (AKJV)

# David Serves King Saul

## 1 Samuel 16

NOW THE SPIRIT of the LORD had left Saul, and the LORD sent a tormenting spirit that filled him with depression and fear.

Some of Saul's servants said to him, "A tormenting spirit from God is troubling you. Let us find a good musician to play the harp whenever the tormenting spirit troubles you. He will play soothing music, and you will soon be well again."

"All right," Saul said. "Find me someone who plays well, and bring him here."

One of the servants said to Saul, "One of Jesse's sons from Bethlehem is a talented harp player. Not only that—he is a brave warrior, a man of war, and has good judgment. He is also a fine-looking young man, and the LORD is with him."

So Saul sent messengers to Jesse to say, "Send me your son David, the shepherd." Jesse responded by sending David to Saul, along with a young goat, a donkey loaded with bread, and a wineskin full of wine.

So David went to Saul and began serving him. Saul loved David very much, and David became his armor bearer.

Then Saul sent word to Jesse asking, "Please let David remain in my service, for I am very pleased with him."

And whenever the tormenting spirit from God troubled Saul, David would play the harp. Then Saul would feel better, and the tormenting spirit would go away.

1 Samuel 16:14–23 (NLT)

# David and Goliath

## 1 Samuel 17

A MAN NAMED GOLIATH, from the city of Gath, came out from the Philistine camp to challenge the Israelites. He was over nine feet tall and wore bronze armor that weighed about 125 pounds and a bronze helmet.

David said to Saul, "Your Majesty, no one should be afraid of this Philistine! I will go and fight him."

"No," answered Saul. "How could you fight him? You're just a boy, and he has been a soldier all his life!"

"Your Majesty," David said, "I take care of my father's sheep. Any time a lion or a bear carries off a lamb, I go after it, attack it, and rescue the lamb. And if the lion or bear turns on me, I grab it by the throat and beat it to death.

"The LORD has saved me from lions and bears; he will save me from this Philistine."

"All right," Saul answered. "Go, and the LORD be with you."

### DAVID DEFEATS GOLIATH

The Philistine started walking toward David, with his shield bearer walking in front of him. When he got a good look at David, he was filled with scorn for him because he was just a nice, good-looking boy. He said to David, "What's that stick for? Do you think I'm a dog?"

David answered, "You are coming against me with sword, spear, and javelin, but I come against you in the name of the LORD Almighty, the God of the Israelite armies, which you have defied."

Goliath started walking toward David again, and David ran quickly toward the Philistine battle line to fight him. He reached into his bag and took out a stone, which he slung at Goliath. It hit him on the forehead and broke his skull, and Goliath fell face downward on the ground. And so, without a sword, David defeated and killed Goliath with a sling and a stone!

1 Samuel 17:4–5, 32–35, 37, 41–43, 45, 48–50 (GNT)

CLEVELAND
WOODWARD

# Saul Is Jealous of David

## 1 Samuel 18

WHEN THE VICTORIOUS Israelite army was returning home after David had killed the Philistine [Goliath], women from all the towns of Israel came out to meet King Saul. They sang and danced for joy with tambourines and cymbals. This was their song:

> "Saul has killed his thousands,
>
> and David his ten thousands!"

This made Saul very angry. "What's this?" he said. "They credit David with ten thousands and me with only thousands. Next they'll be making him their king!" So from that time on Saul kept a jealous eye on David.

The very next day a tormenting spirit from God overwhelmed Saul, and he began to rave in his house like a madman. David was playing the harp, as he did each day. But Saul had a spear in his hand, and he suddenly hurled it at David, intending to pin him to the wall. But David escaped him twice.

Saul was then afraid of David, for the LORD was with David and had turned away from Saul. Finally, Saul sent him away and appointed him commander over 1,000 men, and David faithfully led his troops into battle.

David continued to succeed in everything he did, for the LORD was with him. When Saul recognized this, he became even more afraid of him. But all Israel and Judah loved David because he was so successful at leading his troops into battle.

1 Samuel 18:6–16 (NLT)

# David and Jonathan Are Friends

## 1 Samuel 18 and 19

AFTER DAVID HAD FINISHED talking with Saul, he met Jonathan, the king's son. There was an immediate bond between them, for Jonathan loved David. From that day on Saul kept David with him and wouldn't let him return home. And Jonathan made a solemn pact with David, because he loved him as he loved himself. Jonathan sealed the pact by taking off his robe and giving it to David, together with his tunic, sword, bow, and belt.

### SAUL TRIES TO KILL DAVID

Saul now urged his servants and his son Jonathan to assassinate David. But Jonathan, because of his strong affection for David, told him what his father was planning. "Tomorrow morning," he warned him, "you must find a hiding place out in the fields. I'll ask my father to go out there with me, and I'll talk to him about you. Then I'll tell you everything I can find out."

The next morning Jonathan spoke with his father about David, saying many good things about him. "The king must not sin against his servant David," Jonathan said. "He's never done anything to harm you. He has always helped you in any way he could. Have you forgotten about the time he risked his life to kill the Philistine giant and how the LORD brought a great victory to all Israel as a result? You were certainly happy about it then. Why should you murder an innocent man like David? There is no reason for it at all!"

So Saul listened to Jonathan and vowed, "As surely as the LORD lives, David will not be killed."

Afterward Jonathan called David and told him what had happened. Then he brought David to Saul, and David served in the court as before.

1 Samuel 18:1–4; 19:1–7 (NLT)

# Jonathan Helps David

## 1 Samuel 20

DAVID RAN FROM NAIOTH in Ramah, and came and said to Jonathan, "What have I done? What is my sin? What have I done wrong to your father, that he wants to kill me?"

Then Jonathan said to David, "Tomorrow is the new moon. You will be missed because your seat will be empty. On the third day hurry and come to the place where you hid yourself the other time. Stay by the stone called Ezel. I will shoot three arrows to the side of it, as if I shot at a mark. Then I will send the boy, saying, 'Go, find the arrows.' If I say to the boy these words, 'See, the arrows are on this side of you, get them!' then you may come. For it is safe for you and there is no danger, as the Lord lives. But if I say to the boy, 'See, the arrows are farther away,' then go, for the Lord has sent you away."

In the morning Jonathan went out to the field at the time he and David agreed to meet. A little boy was with him. Jonathan said to his boy, "Run, find the arrows I shoot." As the boy was running, he shot an arrow past him. The boy came to the place where Jonathan had shot the arrow. Jonathan called to the boy and said, "Is not the arrow farther away?" Jonathan called to the boy, "Hurry, be quick, do not stay!" Then Jonathan's boy picked up the arrow and came to his owner. The boy knew nothing. Only Jonathan and David knew what had happened. Then Jonathan gave his bow and arrows to his boy and told him, "Go, take them to the city." When the boy was gone, David rose from the south side and fell on his face to the ground. He bowed three times. Jonathan said to David, "Go in peace. For we have promised each other in the name of the Lord, saying, 'The Lord will be between me and you, and between my children and your children forever.'" Then David got up and left, and Jonathan went into the city.

1 Samuel 20:1, 18–22, 35–42 (NLV)

# David Spares Saul's Life

## 1 Samuel 26

NOW SOME MEN FROM ZIPH came to Saul at Gibeah to tell him, "David is hiding on the hill of Hakilah, which overlooks Jeshimon."

So Saul took 3,000 of Israel's elite troops and went to hunt him down in the wilderness of Ziph. Saul camped along the road beside the hill of Hakilah, near Jeshimon, where David was hiding. When David learned that Saul had come after him into the wilderness, he sent out spies to verify the report of Saul's arrival.

David slipped over to Saul's camp one night to look around. Saul and Abner son of Ner, the commander of his army, were sleeping inside a ring formed by the slumbering warriors. "Who will volunteer to go in there with me?" David asked Ahimelech the Hittite and Abishai son of Zeruiah, Joab's brother.

"I'll go with you," Abishai replied. So David and Abishai went right into Saul's camp and found him asleep, with his spear stuck in the ground beside his head. Abner and the soldiers were lying asleep around him.

"God has surely handed your enemy over to you this time!" Abishai whispered to David. "Let me pin him to the ground with one thrust of the spear; I won't need to strike twice!"

"No!" David said. "Don't kill him. For who can remain innocent after attacking the LORD's anointed one? Surely the LORD will strike Saul down someday, or he will die of old age or in battle. The LORD forbid that I should kill the one he has anointed! But take his spear and that jug of water beside his head, and then let's get out of here!"

1 Samuel 26:1–11 (NLT)

# David Anointed King

## 2 Samuel 1, 2, and 5

David had defeated the Amalekites and returned to Ziklag. Three days later, a soldier came from Saul's army. His clothes were torn, and dirt was on his head. He went to David and knelt down in front of him.

David asked, "Where did you come from?"

The man answered, "From Israel's army. I barely escaped with my life."

"Who won the battle?" David asked.

The man said, "Our army turned and ran, but many were wounded and died. Even King Saul and his son Jonathan are dead."

Right away, David and his soldiers tore their clothes in sorrow. They cried all day long and would not eat anything. Everyone was sad because Saul, his son Jonathan, and many of the Lord's people had been killed in the battle.

Later, David asked the Lord, "Should I go back to one of the towns of Judah?"

The Lord answered, "Yes."

David asked, "Which town should I go to?"

"Go to Hebron," the Lord replied.

The people of Judah met with David at Hebron and poured olive oil on his head to show that he was their new king.

Israel's leaders met with David at Hebron and said, "We are your relatives. Even when Saul was king, you led our nation in battle. And the Lord promised that someday you would rule Israel and take care of us like a shepherd."

Then the leaders poured olive oil on David's head to show that he was now the king of Israel.

2 Samuel 1:1–4, 11–12; 2:1, 4; 5:1–3 (CEV)

# Moving the Ark to Jerusalem

## 2 Samuel 6

DAVID AND ALL THE HOUSE of Israel were celebrating before the LORD, with songs and lyres and harps and tambourines and castanets and cymbals. And when they came to the threshing floor of Nacon, Uzzah put out his hand to the ark of God and took hold of it, for the oxen stumbled. And the anger of the LORD was kindled against Uzzah, and God struck him down there because of his error, and he died there beside the ark of God. And David was angry because the LORD had broken out against Uzzah. And that place is called Perez-uzzah to this day. And David was afraid of the LORD that day, and he said, "How can the ark of the LORD come to me?" So David was not willing to take the ark of the LORD into the city of David. But David took it aside to the house of Obed-edom the Gittite. And the ark of the LORD remained in the house of Obed-edom the Gittite three months, and the LORD blessed Obed-edom and all his household.

And it was told King David, "The LORD has blessed the household of Obed-edom and all that belongs to him, because of the ark of God." So David went and brought up the ark of God from the house of Obed-edom to the city of David with rejoicing.

2 Samuel 6:5–12 (ESV)

# David Keeps a Promise

## 2 Samuel 9

THERE WAS A SERVANT of Saul's family named Ziba, and he was told to go to David. "Are you Ziba?" the king asked.

"At your service, sir," he answered.

The king asked him, "Is there anyone left of Saul's family to whom I can show loyalty and kindness, as I promised God I would?"

Ziba answered, "There is still one of Jonathan's sons. He is crippled."

So King David sent for him.

When Mephibosheth, the son of Jonathan and grandson of Saul, arrived, he bowed down before David in respect. David said, "Mephibosheth," and he answered, "At your service, sir."

"Don't be afraid," David replied. "I will be kind to you for the sake of your father Jonathan. I will give you back all the land that belonged to your grandfather Saul, and you will always be welcome at my table."

Mephibosheth bowed again and said, "I am no better than a dead dog, sir! Why should you be so good to me?"

Then the king called Ziba, Saul's servant, and said, "I am giving Mephibosheth, your master's grandson, everything that belonged to Saul and his family. You, your sons, and your servants will farm the land for your master Saul's family and bring in the harvest, to provide food for them. But Mephibosheth himself will always be a guest at my table."

Ziba answered, "I will do everything Your Majesty commands."

So Mephibosheth ate at the king's table, just like one of the king's sons. Mephibosheth had a young son named Mica. All the members of Ziba's family became servants of Mephibosheth. So Mephibosheth, who was crippled in both feet, lived in Jerusalem, eating all his meals at the king's table.

2 Samuel 9:2–3, 5–13 (GNT)

# Solomon Becomes King

## 1 Kings 1

KING DAVID WAS NOW AN OLD MAN.

Adonijah was the son of David and Haggith. He was Absalom's younger brother and was very handsome. One day, Adonijah started bragging, "I'm going to make myself king!" So he got some chariots and horses, and he hired fifty men as bodyguards. David did not want to hurt his feelings, so he never asked Adonijah why he was doing these things.

Adonijah invited his brothers and David's officials from Judah to go with him to Crawling Rock near Rogel Spring, where he sacrificed some sheep, cattle, and fat calves. But he did not invite Nathan, Benaiah, David's bodyguards, or his own brother Solomon.

When Nathan heard what had happened, he asked Bathsheba, Solomon's mother:

> Have you heard that Adonijah the son of Haggith has made himself king? But David doesn't know a thing about it. You and your son Solomon will be killed, unless you do what I tell you. Go say to David, "You promised me that Solomon would be the next king. So why is Adonijah now king?"

David said, "Tell Bathsheba to come here." She came and stood in front of him. Then he said, "The living LORD God of Israel has kept me safe. And so today, I will keep the promise I made to you in his name: Solomon will be the next king!"

Then David said, "Tell Zadok, Nathan, and Benaiah to come here."

When they arrived, he told them:

> Take along some of my officials and have Solomon ride my own mule to Gihon Spring. When you get there, Zadok and Nathan will make Solomon the new king of Israel. Bring him back here, and he will take my place as king. He is the one I have chosen to rule Israel and Judah.

1 Kings 1:1, 5–6, 9–13, 28–30, 32–35 (CEV)

# Solomon Told to Build God's Temple

## 1 Chronicles 22

DAVID SENT FOR HIS SON Solomon and told him to build a temple for the LORD God of Israel. He said:

> My son, I wanted to build a temple where the LORD my God would be worshiped. But some time ago, he told me, "David, you have killed too many people and have fought too many battles. That's why you are not the one to build my temple. But when your son becomes king, I will give him peace throughout his kingdom. His name will be Solomon, because during his rule I will keep Israel safe and peaceful. Solomon will build my temple. He will be like a son to me, and I will be like a father to him. In fact, one of his descendants will always rule in Israel."
>
> Solomon, my son, I now pray that the LORD your God will be with you and keep his promise to help you build a temple for him. May he give you wisdom and knowledge, so that you can rule Israel according to his Law. If you obey the laws and teachings that the LORD gave Moses, you will be successful. Be strong and brave and don't get discouraged or be afraid of anything.

1 Chronicles 22:6–13 (CEV)

# Solomon Asks for Wisdom

## 1 Kings 3

SOLOMON LOVED the LORD and followed all the decrees of his father, David, except that Solomon, too, offered sacrifices and burned incense at the local places of worship. The most important of these places of worship was at Gibeon, so the king went there and sacrificed 1,000 burnt offerings. That night the LORD appeared to Solomon in a dream, and God said, "What do you want? Ask, and I will give it to you!"

Solomon replied, "You showed great and faithful love to your servant my father, David, because he was honest and true and faithful to you. And you have continued to show this great and faithful love to him today by giving him a son to sit on his throne.

"Now, O LORD my God, you have made me king instead of my father, David, but I am like a little child who doesn't know his way around. And here I am in the midst of your own chosen people, a nation so great and numerous they cannot be counted! Give me an understanding heart so that I can govern your people well and know the difference between right and wrong. For who by himself is able to govern this great people of yours?"

The Lord was pleased that Solomon had asked for wisdom. So God replied, "Because you have asked for wisdom in governing my people with justice and have not asked for a long life or wealth or the death of your enemies—I will give you what you asked for! I will give you a wise and understanding heart such as no one else has had or ever will have! And I will also give you what you did not ask for—riches and fame! No other king in all the world will be compared to you for the rest of your life!"

1 Kings 3:3–13 (NLT)

# Solomon Settles an Argument

## 1 Kings 3

ONE DAY TWO WOMEN came to King Solomon, and one of them said:

> Your Majesty, this woman and I live in the same house. Not long ago my baby was born at home, and three days later her baby was born. Nobody else was there with us.
>
> One night while we were all asleep, she rolled over on her baby, and he died. Then while I was still asleep, she got up and took my son out of my bed. She put him in her bed, then she put her dead baby next to me.
>
> In the morning when I got up to feed my son, I saw that he was dead. But when I looked at him in the light, I knew he wasn't my son.

"No!" the other woman shouted. "He was your son. My baby is alive!"

"The dead baby is yours," the first woman yelled. "Mine is alive!"

They argued back and forth in front of Solomon, until finally he said, "Both of you say this live baby is yours. Someone bring me a sword."

A sword was brought, and Solomon ordered, "Cut the baby in half! That way each of you can have part of him."

"Please don't kill my son," the baby's mother screamed. "Your Majesty, I love him very much, but give him to her. Just don't kill him."

The other woman shouted, "Go ahead and cut him in half. Then neither of us will have the baby."

Solomon said, "Don't kill the baby." Then he pointed to the first woman, "She is his real mother. Give the baby to her."

Everyone in Israel was amazed when they heard how Solomon had made his decision. They realized that God had given him wisdom to judge fairly.

1 Kings 3:16–28 (CEV)

# The Temple in Jerusalem

## 2 Chronicles 6

THEN SOLOMON PRAYED, "O LORD, you have said that you would live in a thick cloud of darkness. Now I have built a glorious Temple for you, a place where you can live forever!"

Then the king turned around to the entire community of Israel standing before him and gave this blessing: "Praise the LORD, the God of Israel, who has kept the promise he made to my father, David. For he told my father, 'From the day I brought my people out of the land of Egypt, I have never chosen a city among any of the tribes of Israel as the place where a Temple should be built to honor my name. Nor have I chosen a king to lead my people Israel. But now I have chosen Jerusalem as the place for my name to be honored, and I have chosen David to be king over my people Israel.'"

Then Solomon said, "My father, David, wanted to build this Temple to honor the name of the LORD, the God of Israel. But the LORD told him, 'You wanted to build the Temple to honor my name. Your intention is good, but you are not the one to do it. One of your own sons will build the Temple to honor me.'

"And now the LORD has fulfilled the promise he made, for I have become king in my father's place, and now I sit on the throne of Israel, just as the LORD promised. I have built this Temple to honor the name of the LORD, the God of Israel."

2 Chronicles 6:1–10 (NLT)

# Solomon Dedicates the Temple

## 1 Kings 8

SOLOMON STOOD before the altar of the LORD in front of the entire community of Israel. He lifted his hands toward heaven, and he prayed,

"O LORD, God of Israel, there is no God like you in all of heaven above or on the earth below. You keep your covenant and show unfailing love to all who walk before you in wholehearted devotion. You have kept your promise to your servant David, my father. You made that promise with your own mouth, and with your own hands you have fulfilled it today.

"And now, O LORD, God of Israel, carry out the additional promise you made to your servant David, my father. For you said to him, 'If your descendants guard their behavior and faithfully follow me as you have done, one of them will always sit on the throne of Israel.' Now, O God of Israel, fulfill this promise to your servant David, my father.

"But will God really live on earth? Why, even the highest heavens cannot contain you. How much less this Temple I have built! Nevertheless, listen to my prayer and my plea, O LORD my God. Hear the cry and the prayer that your servant is making to you today. May you watch over this Temple night and day, this place where you have said, 'My name will be there.' May you always hear the prayers I make toward this place. May you hear the humble and earnest requests from me and your people Israel when we pray toward this place. Yes, hear us from heaven where you live, and when you hear, forgive."

1 Kings 8:22–30 (NLT)

# The Queen of Sheba Visits Solomon

## 1 Kings 10

WHEN THE QUEEN OF SHEBA heard of Solomon's fame, which brought honor to the name of the LORD, she came to test him with hard questions. She arrived in Jerusalem with a large group of attendants and a great caravan of camels loaded with spices, large quantities of gold, and precious jewels. When she met with Solomon, she talked with him about everything she had on her mind. Solomon had answers for all her questions; nothing was too hard for the king to explain to her. When the queen of Sheba realized how very wise Solomon was, and when she saw the palace he had built, she was overwhelmed. She was also amazed at the food on his tables, the organization of his officials and their splendid clothing, the cup-bearers, and the burnt offerings Solomon made at the Temple of the LORD.

She exclaimed to the king, "Everything I heard in my country about your achievements and wisdom is true! I didn't believe what was said until I arrived here and saw it with my own eyes. In fact, I had not heard the half of it! Your wisdom and prosperity are far beyond what I was told. How happy your people must be! What a privilege for your officials to stand here day after day, listening to your wisdom! Praise the LORD your God, who delights in you and has placed you on the throne of Israel. Because of the LORD's eternal love for Israel, he has made you king so you can rule with justice and righteousness."

King Solomon gave the queen of Sheba whatever she asked for, besides all the customary gifts he had so generously given. Then she and all her attendants returned to their own land.

1 Kings 10:1–9, 13 (NLT)

# Elijah the Prophet

## 1 Kings 16 and 17

AHAB SON OF OMRI began to rule over Israel in the thirty-eighth year of King Asa's reign in Judah. He reigned in Samaria twenty-two years. But Ahab son of Omri did what was evil in the LORD's sight, even more than any of the kings before him.

### ELIJAH FED BY RAVENS

Now Elijah, who was from Tishbe in Gilead, told King Ahab, "As surely as the LORD, the God of Israel, lives—the God I serve—there will be no dew or rain during the next few years until I give the word!"

Then the LORD said to Elijah, "Go to the east and hide by Kerith Brook, near where it enters the Jordan River. Drink from the brook and eat what the ravens bring you, for I have commanded them to bring you food."

So Elijah did as the LORD told him and camped beside Kerith Brook, east of the Jordan. The ravens brought him bread and meat each morning and evening, and he drank from the brook. But after a while the brook dried up, for there was no rainfall anywhere in the land.

1 Kings 16:29–30; 17:1–7 (NLT)

# Elijah Helps a Widow

## 1 Kings 17

THE LORD SAID TO ELIJAH, "Go and live in the village of Zarephath, near the city of Sidon. I have instructed a widow there to feed you."

So he went to Zarephath. As he arrived at the gates of the village, he saw a widow gathering sticks, and he asked her, "Would you please bring me a little water in a cup?" As she was going to get it, he called to her, "Bring me a bite of bread, too."

But she said, "I swear by the LORD your God that I don't have a single piece of bread in the house. And I have only a handful of flour left in the jar and a little cooking oil in the bottom of the jug. I was just gathering a few sticks to cook this last meal, and then my son and I will die."

But Elijah said to her, "Don't be afraid! Go ahead and do just what you've said, but make a little bread for me first. Then use what's left to prepare a meal for yourself and your son. For this is what the LORD, the God of Israel, says: There will always be flour and olive oil left in your containers until the time when the LORD sends rain and the crops grow again!"

So she did as Elijah said, and she and Elijah and her family continued to eat for many days. There was always enough flour and olive oil left in the containers, just as the LORD had promised through Elijah.

1 Kings 17:8–16 (NLT)

# Elijah Heals the Widow's Son

## 1 Kings 17

THEN THE LORD SAID TO ELIJAH, "Go and live in the village of Zarephath, near the city of Sidon. I have instructed a widow there to feed you."

Some time later the woman's son became sick. He grew worse and worse, and finally he died. Then she said to Elijah, "O man of God, what have you done to me? Have you come here to point out my sins and kill my son?"

But Elijah replied, "Give me your son." And he took the child's body from her arms, carried him up the stairs to the room where he was staying, and laid the body on his bed. Then Elijah cried out to the LORD, "O LORD my God, why have you brought tragedy to this widow who has opened her home to me, causing her son to die?"

And he stretched himself out over the child three times and cried out to the LORD, "O LORD my God, please let this child's life return to him." The LORD heard Elijah's prayer, and the life of the child returned, and he revived! Then Elijah brought him down from the upper room and gave him to his mother. "Look!" he said. "Your son is alive!"

Then the woman told Elijah, "Now I know for sure that you are a man of God, and that the LORD truly speaks through you."

1 Kings 17:8–9, 17–24 (NLT)

# Elijah Versus the Prophets of Baal

## 1 Kings 18

So AHAB SUMMONED ALL THE ISRAELITES and the prophets of Baal to meet at Mount Carmel. Elijah went up to the people and said, "If the LORD is God, worship him; but if Baal is God, worship him!" Then Elijah said, "Then let the prophets of Baal pray to their god, and I will pray to the LORD, and the one who answers by sending fire—he is God."

The people shouted their approval.

They took the bull that was brought to them, prepared it, and prayed to Baal until noon. They shouted, "Answer us, Baal!" and kept dancing around the altar they had built. But no answer came.

Then Elijah said to the people, "Come closer to me," and they all gathered around him. He set about repairing the altar of the LORD which had been torn down.

Then he placed the wood on the altar, cut the bull in pieces, and laid it on the wood. He said, "Fill four jars with water and pour it on the offering and the wood." They did so, and he said, "Do it again"—and they did. "Do it once more," he said—and they did. The water ran down around the altar and filled the trench.

At the hour of the afternoon sacrifice the prophet Elijah approached the altar and prayed, "O LORD, the God of Abraham, Isaac, and Jacob, prove now that you are the God of Israel and that I am your servant and have done all this at your command. Answer me, LORD, answer me, so that this people will know that you, the LORD, are God and that you are bringing them back to yourself."

The LORD sent fire down, and it burned up the sacrifice, the wood, and the stones, scorched the earth and dried up the water in the trench. When the people saw this, they threw themselves on the ground and exclaimed, "The LORD is God; the LORD alone is God!"

1 Kings 18:20–22, 24, 26, 30, 33–39 (GNT)

# An Angel Helps Elijah

## 1 Kings 19

WHEN AHAB GOT HOME, he told Jezebel everything Elijah had done, including the way he had killed all the prophets of Baal. So Jezebel sent this message to Elijah: "May the gods strike me and even kill me if by this time tomorrow I have not killed you just as you killed them."

Elijah was afraid and fled for his life. He went to Beersheba, a town in Judah, and he left his servant there. Then he went on alone into the wilderness, traveling all day. He sat down under a solitary broom tree and prayed that he might die. "I have had enough, LORD," he said. "Take my life, for I am no better than my ancestors who have already died."

Then he lay down and slept under the broom tree. But as he was sleeping, an angel touched him and told him, "Get up and eat!" He looked around and there beside his head was some bread baked on hot stones and a jar of water! So he ate and drank and lay down again.

Then the angel of the LORD came again and touched him and said, "Get up and eat some more, or the journey ahead will be too much for you."

So he got up and ate and drank, and the food gave him enough strength to travel forty days and forty nights to Mount Sinai, the mountain of God. There he came to a cave, where he spent the night.

1 Kings 19:1–9 (NLT)

# Elisha Joins Elijah

## 1 Kings 19

A VOICE SAID, "What are you doing here, Elijah?"

He replied again, "I have zealously served the LORD God Almighty. But the people of Israel have broken their covenant with you, torn down your altars, and killed every one of your prophets. I am the only one left, and now they are trying to kill me, too."

Then the LORD told him, "Go back the same way you came, and travel to the wilderness of Damascus. When you arrive there, anoint Hazael to be king of Aram. Then anoint Jehu grandson of Nimshi to be king of Israel, and anoint Elisha son of Shaphat from the town of Abel-meholah to replace you as my prophet. Anyone who escapes from Hazael will be killed by Jehu, and those who escape Jehu will be killed by Elisha! Yet I will preserve 7,000 others in Israel who have never bowed down to Baal or kissed him!"

### THE CALL OF ELISHA

So Elijah went and found Elisha son of Shaphat plowing a field. There were twelve teams of oxen in the field, and Elisha was plowing with the twelfth team. Elijah went over to him and threw his cloak across his shoulders and then walked away. Elisha left the oxen standing there, ran after Elijah, and said to him, "First let me go and kiss my father and mother good-bye, and then I will go with you!"

Elijah replied, "Go on back, but think about what I have done to you."

So Elisha returned to his oxen and slaughtered them. He used the wood from the plow to build a fire to roast their flesh. He passed around the meat to the townspeople, and they all ate. Then he went with Elijah as his assistant.

1 Kings 19:13–21 (NLT)

DWARD.

# Elijah Taken Up to Heaven

## 2 Kings 2

WHEN THE LORD was about to take Elijah up to heaven by a wind-storm, Elijah and Elisha were on their way from Gilgal.

Then Elijah said to him, "I ask you to stay here. For the Lord has sent me to the Jordan." And Elisha said, "As the Lord lives and as you yourself live, I will not leave you." So the two of them went on.

Then Elijah took his coat and rolled it up and hit the water. And the water divided to one side and to the other, so the two of them crossed the Jordan on dry ground. When they had crossed, Elijah said to Elisha, "Ask what I should do for you before I am taken from you." And Elisha said, "I ask you, let twice the share of your spirit be upon me." Elijah said, "You have asked a hard thing. But if you see me when I am taken from you, it will be given to you. But if not, it will not be so." As they went on and talked, a war-wagon of fire and horses of fire came between them. And Elijah went up by a wind-storm to heaven. Elisha saw it and cried out, "My father, my father, the war-wagon of Israel and its horsemen!" And he saw Elijah no more. Then he took hold of his own clothes and tore them in two pieces. He picked up Elijah's coat that had fallen from him. And he returned and stood by the side of the Jordan. He took Elijah's coat that fell from him, and hit the water and said, "Where is the Lord, the God of Elijah?" When he hit the water, it was divided to one side and to the other, and Elisha crossed the Jordan.

2 Kings 2:1, 6, 8–14 (NLV)

# Elisha and the Widow's Oil

## 2 Kings 4

ONE DAY THE WIDOW of a member of the group of prophets came to Elisha and cried out, "My husband who served you is dead, and you know how he feared the LORD. But now a creditor has come, threatening to take my two sons as slaves."

"What can I do to help you?" Elisha asked. "Tell me, what do you have in the house?"

"Nothing at all, except a flask of olive oil," she replied.

And Elisha said, "Borrow as many empty jars as you can from your friends and neighbors. Then go into your house with your sons and shut the door behind you. Pour olive oil from your flask into the jars, setting each one aside when it is filled."

So she did as she was told. Her sons kept bringing jars to her, and she filled one after another. Soon every container was full to the brim!

"Bring me another jar," she said to one of her sons.

"There aren't any more!" he told her. And then the olive oil stopped flowing.

When she told the man of God what had happened, he said to her, "Now sell the olive oil and pay your debts, and you and your sons can live on what is left over."

2 Kings 4:1–7 (NLT)

# Elisha and the Shunammite Woman

## 2 Kings 4

ONE DAY ELISHA went to the town of Shunem. A wealthy woman lived there, and she urged him to come to her home for a meal. After that, whenever he passed that way, he would stop there for something to eat.

She said to her husband, "I am sure this man who stops in from time to time is a holy man of God. Let's build a small room for him on the roof and furnish it with a bed, a table, a chair, and a lamp. Then he will have a place to stay whenever he comes by."

One day Elisha returned to Shunem, and he went up to this upper room to rest. He said to his servant Gehazi, "Tell the woman from Shunem I want to speak to her." When she appeared, Elisha said to Gehazi, "Tell her, 'We appreciate the kind concern you have shown us. What can we do for you? Can we put in a good word for you to the king or to the commander of the army?'"

"No," she replied, "my family takes good care of me."

Later Elisha asked Gehazi, "What can we do for her?"

Gehazi replied, "She doesn't have a son, and her husband is an old man."

"Call her back again," Elisha told him. When the woman returned, Elisha said to her as she stood in the doorway, "Next year at this time you will be holding a son in your arms!"

"No, my lord!" she cried. "O man of God, don't deceive me and get my hopes up like that."

But sure enough, the woman soon became pregnant. And at that time the following year she had a son, just as Elisha had said.

2 Kings 4:8–17 (NLT)

# Elisha Heals the Shunammite's Son

## 2 Kings 4

WHEN THE [Shunammite woman's] child was grown, he went out one day to his father who was with those gathering grain. He said to his father, "O, my head, my head!" The father said to his servant, "Carry him to his mother." When he was brought to his mother, he sat on her knees until noon. Then he died.

So she went and came to the man of God at Mount Carmel.

Then she said, "Did I ask you for a son? Did I not say, 'Do not lie to me'?"

Elisha said to Gehazi, "Get ready to travel. Take my walking stick and go. If you meet any man, do not greet him. If anyone greets you, do not answer him. Then lay my stick on the boy's face." The mother of the boy said, "As the Lord lives and as you yourself live, I will not leave you." So Elisha got up and followed her.

When Elisha came into the house, he saw the boy lying dead on his bed. So he went in and shut the door behind the two of them, and prayed to the Lord. He went up and lay on the child. He put his mouth on his mouth, and his eyes on his eyes, and his hands on his hands. He spread himself out on him, and the child's flesh became warm. Then Elisha got up again. He walked from one end of the house to the other. Then he went up and spread himself on the child again. The boy sneezed seven times, and opened his eyes. Elisha called Gehazi and said, "Call this Shunammite." So he called her. When she came to him, he said, "Take up your son." She came and fell at his feet and put her face to the ground. Then she took up her son and went out.

2 Kings 4:18–20, 25, 28–30, 32–37 (NLV)

# A Hebrew Maiden Offers a Solution

## 2 Kings 5

THE KING OF ARAM had great admiration for Naaman, the commander of his army, because through him the LORD had given Aram great victories. But though Naaman was a mighty warrior, he suffered from leprosy.

At this time Aramean raiders had invaded the land of Israel, and among their captives was a young girl who had been given to Naaman's wife as a maid. One day the girl said to her mistress, "I wish my master would go to see the prophet in Samaria. He would heal him of his leprosy."

So Naaman told the king what the young girl from Israel had said. "Go and visit the prophet," the king of Aram told him. "I will send a letter of introduction for you to take to the king of Israel." So Naaman started out, carrying as gifts 750 pounds of silver, 150 pounds of gold, and ten sets of clothing. The letter to the king of Israel said: "With this letter I present my servant Naaman. I want you to heal him of his leprosy."

When the king of Israel read the letter, he tore his clothes in dismay and said, "Am I God, that I can give life and take it away? Why is this man asking me to heal someone with leprosy? I can see that he's just trying to pick a fight with me."

But when Elisha, the man of God, heard that the king of Israel had torn his clothes in dismay, he sent this message to him: "Why are you so upset? Send Naaman to me, and he will learn that there is a true prophet here in Israel."

2 Kings 5:1–8 (NLT)

# Naaman Is Thankful for Healing

## 2 Kings 5

SO NAAMAN WENT WITH HIS HORSES and chariots and waited at the door of Elisha's house. But Elisha sent a messenger out to him with this message: "Go and wash yourself seven times in the Jordan River. Then your skin will be restored, and you will be healed of your leprosy."

But Naaman became angry and stalked away. "I thought he would certainly come out to meet me!" he said. "I expected him to wave his hand over the leprosy and call on the name of the LORD his God and heal me! Aren't the rivers of Damascus, the Abana and the Pharpar, better than any of the rivers of Israel? Why shouldn't I wash in them and be healed?" So Naaman turned and went away in a rage.

But his officers tried to reason with him and said, "Sir, if the prophet had told you to do something very difficult, wouldn't you have done it? So you should certainly obey him when he says simply, 'Go and wash and be cured!'" So Naaman went down to the Jordan River and dipped himself seven times, as the man of God had instructed him. And his skin became as healthy as the skin of a young child, and he was healed!

Then Naaman and his entire party went back to find the man of God. They stood before him, and Naaman said, "Now I know that there is no God in all the world except in Israel. So please accept a gift from your servant."

But Elisha replied, "As surely as the LORD lives, whom I serve, I will not accept any gifts." And though Naaman urged him to take the gift, Elisha refused.

2 Kings 5:9–16 (NLT)

# Elisha's Heavenly Defenders

## 2 Kings 6

WHEN THE KING OF ARAM was at war with Israel, he would confer with his officers and say, "We will mobilize our forces at such and such a place."

But immediately Elisha, the man of God, would warn the king of Israel, "Do not go near that place, for the Arameans are planning to mobilize their troops there." So the king of Israel would send word to the place indicated by the man of God. Time and again Elisha warned the king, so that he would be on the alert there.

The king of Aram became very upset over this. He called his officers together and demanded, "Which of you is the traitor? Who has been informing the king of Israel of my plans?"

"It's not us, my lord the king," one of the officers replied. "Elisha, the prophet in Israel, tells the king of Israel even the words you speak in the privacy of your bedroom!"

"Go and find out where he is," the king commanded, "so I can send troops to seize him."

And the report came back: "Elisha is at Dothan." So one night the king of Aram sent a great army with many chariots and horses to surround the city.

When the servant of the man of God got up early the next morning and went outside, there were troops, horses, and chariots everywhere. "Oh, sir, what will we do now?" the young man cried to Elisha.

"Don't be afraid!" Elisha told him. "For there are more on our side than on theirs!" Then Elisha prayed, "O LORD, open his eyes and let him see!" The LORD opened the young man's eyes, and when he looked up, he saw that the hillside around Elisha was filled with horses and chariots of fire.

2 Kings 6:8–17 (NLT)

# Jonah Tries to Run from God

## Jonah 1

ONE DAY THE LORD told Jonah, the son of Amittai, to go to the great city of Nineveh and say to the people, "The LORD has seen your terrible sins. You are doomed!"

Instead, Jonah ran from the LORD. He went to the seaport of Joppa and bought a ticket on a ship that was going to Spain. Then he got on the ship and sailed away to escape.

But the LORD made a strong wind blow, and such a bad storm came up that the ship was about to be broken to pieces. The sailors were frightened, and they all started praying to their gods. They even threw the ship's cargo overboard to make the ship lighter.

All this time, Jonah was down below deck, sound asleep. The ship's captain went to him and said, "How can you sleep at a time like this? Get up and pray to your God! Maybe he will have pity on us and keep us from drowning."

Finally, the sailors got together and said, "Let's ask our gods to show us who caused all this trouble." It turned out to be Jonah.

They started asking him, "Are you the one who brought all this trouble on us? What business are you in? Where do you come from? What is your country? Who are your people?"

Jonah answered, "I'm a Hebrew, and I worship the LORD God of heaven, who made the sea and the dry land."

When the sailors heard this, they were frightened, because Jonah had already told them he was running from the LORD. Then they said, "Do you know what you have done?"

The storm kept getting worse, until finally the sailors asked him, "What should we do with you to make the sea calm down?"

Jonah 1:1–11 (CEV)

# Jonah and the Big Fish

## Jonah 1 and 2

"THROW ME INTO THE SEA," Jonah said, "and it will become calm again. I know that this terrible storm is all my fault."

Instead, the sailors rowed even harder to get the ship to the land. But the stormy sea was too violent for them, and they couldn't make it. Then they cried out to the LORD, Jonah's God. "O LORD," they pleaded, "don't make us die for this man's sin. And don't hold us responsible for his death. O LORD, you have sent this storm upon him for your own good reasons."

Then the sailors picked Jonah up and threw him into the raging sea, and the storm stopped at once! The sailors were awestruck by the LORD's great power, and they offered him a sacrifice and vowed to serve him.

Now the LORD had arranged for a great fish to swallow Jonah. And Jonah was inside the fish for three days and three nights.

### JONAH'S PRAYER

Then Jonah prayed to the LORD his God from inside the fish. He said,

> "I cried out to the LORD in my great trouble,
> and he answered me.
>
> I called to you from the land of the dead,
> and LORD, you heard me!"

Then the LORD ordered the fish to spit Jonah out onto the beach.

Jonah 1:12–17; 2:1–2, 10 (NLT)

CLEVELAND
WOODWARD

# Jonah Goes to Nineveh

## Jonah 3

THEN THE LORD spoke to Jonah a second time: "Get up and go to the great city of Nineveh, and deliver the message I have given you."

This time Jonah obeyed the LORD's command and went to Nineveh, a city so large that it took three days to see it all. On the day Jonah entered the city, he shouted to the crowds: "Forty days from now Nineveh will be destroyed!" The people of Nineveh believed God's message, and from the greatest to the least, they declared a fast and put on burlap to show their sorrow.

When the king of Nineveh heard what Jonah was saying, he stepped down from his throne and took off his royal robes. He dressed himself in burlap and sat on a heap of ashes.

When God saw what they had done and how they had put a stop to their evil ways, he changed his mind and did not carry out the destruction he had threatened.

Jonah 3:1–6, 10 (NLT)

# Jonah Under a Vine

## Jonah 3 and 4

THE PEOPLE of Nineveh believed God's message. So they decided that everyone should fast, and all the people, from the greatest to the least, put on sackcloth to show that they had repented.

God saw what they did; he saw that they had given up their wicked behavior. So he changed his mind and did not punish them as he had said he would.

### JONAH'S ANGER AND GOD'S MERCY

Jonah was very unhappy about this and became angry. So he prayed, "LORD, didn't I say before I left home that this is just what you would do? That's why I did my best to run away to Spain! I knew that you are a loving and merciful God, always patient, always kind, and always ready to change your mind and not punish. Now then, LORD, let me die. I am better off dead than alive."

The LORD answered, "What right do you have to be angry?"

Jonah went out east of the city and sat down. He made a shelter for himself and sat in its shade, waiting to see what would happen to Nineveh. Then the LORD God made a plant grow up over Jonah to give him some shade, so that he would be more comfortable. Jonah was extremely pleased with the plant. But at dawn the next day, at God's command, a worm attacked the plant, and it died. After the sun had risen, God sent a hot east wind, and Jonah was about to faint from the heat of the sun beating down on his head. So he wished he were dead. "I am better off dead than alive," he said.

But God said to him, "What right do you have to be angry about the plant?"

Jonah replied, "I have every right to be angry—angry enough to die!"

The LORD said to him, "This plant grew up in one night and disappeared the next; you didn't do anything for it and you didn't make it grow—yet you feel sorry for it! How much more, then, should I have pity on Nineveh, that great city. After all, it has more than 120,000 innocent children in it, as well as many animals!"

Jonah 3:5, 10; 4:1–11 (GNT)

# A Child Becomes King

## 2 Kings 11 and 12

JOASH WAS SEVEN YEARS OLD when he became king.

### JOASH REPAIRS THE TEMPLE

Joash began to rule over Judah in the seventh year of King Jehu's reign in Israel. He reigned in Jerusalem forty years. His mother was Zibiah from Beersheba. All his life Joash did what was pleasing in the LORD's sight because Jehoiada the priest instructed him. Yet even so, he did not destroy the pagan shrines, and the people still offered sacrifices and burned incense there.

One day King Joash said to the priests, "Collect all the money brought as a sacred offering to the LORD's Temple, whether it is a regular assessment, a payment of vows, or a voluntary gift. Let the priests take some of that money to pay for whatever repairs are needed at the Temple."

But by the twenty-third year of Joash's reign, the priests still had not repaired the Temple. So King Joash called for Jehoiada and the other priests and asked them, "Why haven't you repaired the Temple? Don't use any more money for your own needs. From now on, it must all be spent on Temple repairs." So the priests agreed not to accept any more money from the people, and they also agreed to let others take responsibility for repairing the Temple.

2 Kings 11:21; 12:1–8 (NLT)

# The Kingdom of Israel Falls

## 2 Kings 17

IN THE TWELFTH YEAR of Ahaz king of Judah, Hoshea the son of Elah became the king of Israel in Samaria. He ruled for nine years. Hoshea did what was sinful in the eyes of the Lord, but not as bad as the kings of Israel before him. King Shalmaneser of Assyria came up against him. And Hoshea became his servant and paid taxes to him. But the king of Assyria found that Hoshea had been making plans against him. Hoshea had sent men to King So of Egypt, instead of giving taxes to the king of Assyria. He had done this year after year. So the king of Assyria shut him up and put him in chains in prison.

### ISRAEL CARRIED AWAY TO ASSYRIA

Then the king of Assyria came against all the land. He went up to Samaria and kept soldiers around it for three years. In the ninth year of Hoshea, the king of Assyria took Samaria in battle, and took the people of Israel away to Assyria. He had them live in Halah and Habor, by the river of Gozan, and in the cities of the Medes.

This happened because the people of Israel had sinned against the Lord their God. He had brought them up from the land of Egypt from under the power of Pharaoh, king of Egypt. But they worshiped other gods.

2 Kings 17:1–7 (NLV)

# King Hezekiah Tears Down Idols

## 2 Kings 18

HEZEKIAH SON OF AHAZ began to rule over Judah in the third year of King Hoshea's reign in Israel. He was twenty-five years old when he became king, and he reigned in Jerusalem twenty-nine years. His mother was Abijah, the daughter of Zechariah. He did what was pleasing in the LORD's sight, just as his ancestor David had done. He removed the pagan shrines, smashed the sacred pillars, and cut down the Asherah poles. He broke up the bronze serpent that Moses had made, because the people of Israel had been offering sacrifices to it. The bronze serpent was called Nehushtan.

Hezekiah trusted in the LORD, the God of Israel. There was no one like him among all the kings of Judah, either before or after his time. He remained faithful to the LORD in everything, and he carefully obeyed all the commands the LORD had given Moses. So the LORD was with him, and Hezekiah was successful in everything he did. He revolted against the king of Assyria and refused to pay him tribute. He also conquered the Philistines as far distant as Gaza and its territory, from their smallest outpost to their largest walled city.

2 Kings 18:1–8 (NLT)

CLEVELAND
WOODWARD

# The Kingdom of Judah Falls

## 2 Kings 25

THAT YEAR, which was the nineteenth year of King Nebuchadnezzar's reign, Nebuzaradan, the captain of the guard and an official of the Babylonian king, arrived in Jerusalem. He burned down the Temple of the LORD, the royal palace, and all the houses of Jerusalem. He destroyed all the important buildings in the city. Then he supervised the entire Babylonian army as they tore down the walls of Jerusalem on every side. Then Nebuzaradan, the captain of the guard, took as exiles the rest of the people who remained in the city, the defectors who had declared their allegiance to the king of Babylon, and the rest of the population. But the captain of the guard allowed some of the poorest people to stay behind to care for the vineyards and fields.

The Babylonians broke up the bronze pillars in front of the LORD's Temple, the bronze water carts, and the great bronze basin called the Sea, and they carried all the bronze away to Babylon.

2 Kings 25:8–13 (NLT)

Zingaro

# Daniel Requests Healthy Food

## Daniel 1

IN THE THIRD YEAR that Jehoiakim was king of Judah, King Nebuchadnezzar of Babylonia attacked Jerusalem and surrounded the city. The Lord let him capture King Jehoiakim and seize some of the Temple treasures. He took some prisoners back with him to the temple of his gods in Babylon, and put the captured treasures in the temple storerooms.

The king ordered Ashpenaz, his chief official, to select from among the Israelite exiles some young men of the royal family and of the noble families. They had to be handsome, intelligent, well-trained, quick to learn, and free from physical defects, so that they would be qualified to serve in the royal court. Ashpenaz was to teach them to read and write the Babylonian language. The king also gave orders that every day they were to be given the same food and wine as the members of the royal court. After three years of this training they were to appear before the king.

Daniel made up his mind not to let himself become ritually unclean by eating the food and drinking the wine of the royal court, so he asked Ashpenaz to help him, and God made Ashpenaz sympathetic to Daniel.

"Test us for ten days," he said. "Give us vegetables to eat and water to drink. Then compare us with the young men who are eating the food of the royal court, and base your decision on how we look."

He agreed to let them try it for ten days. When the time was up, they looked healthier and stronger than all those who had been eating the royal food.

Daniel 1:1–5, 8–9, 12–15 (GNT)

# Daniel and Friends Before the King

## Daniel 1

DANIEL, HANANIAH, MISHAEL, AND AZARIAH were four of the young men chosen, all from the tribe of Judah. The chief of staff renamed them with these Babylonian names:

> Daniel was called Belteshazzar.
>
> Hananiah was called Shadrach.
>
> Mishael was called Meshach.
>
> Azariah was called Abednego.

God gave these four young men an unusual aptitude for understanding every aspect of literature and wisdom. And God gave Daniel the special ability to interpret the meanings of visions and dreams.

When the training period ordered by the king was completed, the chief of staff brought all the young men to King Nebuchadnezzar. The king talked with them, and no one impressed him as much as Daniel, Hananiah, Mishael, and Azariah. So they entered the royal service. Whenever the king consulted them in any matter requiring wisdom and balanced judgment, he found them ten times more capable than any of the magicians and enchanters in his entire kingdom.

Daniel remained in the royal service until the first year of the reign of King Cyrus.

Daniel 1:6–7, 17–21 (NLT)

# Three Friends in a Fiery Furnace

## Daniel 3

KING NEBUCHADNEZZAR ordered a gold statue to be built ninety feet high and nine feet wide.

Then an official stood up and announced:

> People of every nation and race, now listen to the king's command! Trumpets, flutes, harps, and all other kinds of musical instruments will soon start playing. When you hear the music, you must bow down and worship the statue that King Nebuchadnezzar has set up. Anyone who refuses will at once be thrown into a flaming furnace.

Some Babylonians used this as a chance to accuse the Jews to King Nebuchadnezzar.

"Those Jews, Shadrach, Meshach, and Abednego, refuse to worship your gods and the statue you have set up."

Nebuchadnezzar's face twisted with anger at the three men. And he ordered the furnace to be heated seven times hotter than usual. Next, he commanded some of his strongest soldiers to tie up the men and throw them into the flaming furnace.

Suddenly the king jumped up and shouted, "Weren't only three men tied up and thrown into the fire?"

"But I see four men walking around in the fire," the king replied. "None of them is tied up or harmed, and the fourth one looks like a god."

Nebuchadnezzar went closer to the flaming furnace and said to the three young men, "You servants of the Most High God, come out at once!"

They came out. The men were not burned, their hair wasn't scorched, and their clothes didn't even smell like smoke. King Nebuchadnezzar said:

> Praise their God for sending an angel to rescue his servants! They trusted their God and refused to obey my commands. Yes, they chose to die rather than to worship or serve any god except their own.

Daniel 3:1, 4–6, 8, 12, 19–20, 24–28 (CEV)

# Nebuchadnezzar's Pride

## Daniel 4

"I, NEBUCHADNEZZAR, was living in my palace in comfort and prosperity. But one night I had a dream that frightened me; I saw visions that terrified me as I lay in my bed.

"At last Daniel came in before me, and I told him the dream.

"Upon hearing this, Daniel (also known as Belteshazzar) was overcome for a time, frightened by the meaning of the dream.

"'This is what the dream means, Your Majesty, and what the Most High has declared will happen to my lord the king. You will be driven from human society, and you will live in the fields with the wild animals. Seven periods of time will pass while you live this way, until you learn that the Most High rules over the kingdoms of the world and gives them to anyone he chooses.'

"But all these things did happen to King Nebuchadnezzar. Twelve months later he was taking a walk on the flat roof of the royal palace in Babylon. As he looked out across the city, he said, 'Look at this great city of Babylon! By my own mighty power, I have built this beautiful city as my royal residence to display my majestic splendor.'

"While these words were still in his mouth, a voice called down from heaven, 'O King Nebuchadnezzar, this message is for you! You are no longer ruler of this kingdom. You will be driven from human society.'

"That same hour the judgment was fulfilled, and Nebuchadnezzar was driven from human society."

### NEBUCHADNEZZAR PRAISES GOD

"After this time had passed, I, Nebuchadnezzar, looked up to heaven. My sanity returned, and I praised and worshiped the Most High and honored the one who lives forever.

"Now I, Nebuchadnezzar, praise and glorify and honor the King of heaven. All his acts are just and true, and he is able to humble the proud."

Daniel 4:4–5, 8, 19, 24–25, 28–32, 33–34, 37 (NLT)

# A Message from God

## Daniel 5

ONE EVENING, KING BELSHAZZAR gave a great banquet for a thousand of his highest officials, and he drank wine with them.

When the gold cups were brought in, everyone at the banquet drank from them and praised their idols made of gold, silver, bronze, iron, wood, and stone.

Suddenly a human hand was seen writing on the plaster wall of the palace.

All of King Belshazzar's highest officials came in, but not one of them could read the writing or tell what it meant, and they were completely puzzled. Now the king was more afraid than ever before, and his face turned white as a ghost.

When the queen heard the king and his officials talking, she came in and said:

> Your Majesty, I hope you live forever! Don't be afraid or look so pale. In your kingdom there is a man who has been given special powers by the holy gods.

When Daniel was brought in, the king said:

> So you are Daniel, one of the captives my father brought back from Judah!
>
> Neither my advisors nor the men who talk with the spirits of the dead could read this writing or tell me what it means. But I have been told that you understand everything and that you can solve difficult problems. Now then, if you can read this writing and tell me what it means, you will become the third most powerful man in my kingdom.

Daniel answered:

> Your Majesty, I will read the writing and tell you what it means.
>
> The words written there are mene, which means "numbered," tekel, which means "weighed," and parsin, which means "divided." God has numbered the days of your kingdom and has brought it to an end. He has weighed you on his balance scales, and you fall short of what it takes to be king. So God has divided your kingdom between the Medes and the Persians.

Daniel 5:1, 3–5, 8–11, 13, 15–17, 25–28 (CEV)

# Daniel Prays

## Daniel 6

DARIUS THE MEDE decided to divide the kingdom into 120 provinces, and he appointed a high officer to rule over each province. The king also chose Daniel and two others as administrators to supervise the high officers and protect the king's interests. Daniel soon proved himself more capable than all the other administrators and high officers. Because of Daniel's great ability, the king made plans to place him over the entire empire.

Then the other administrators and high officers began searching for some fault in the way Daniel was handling government affairs, but they couldn't find anything to criticize or condemn. He was faithful, always responsible, and completely trustworthy. So they concluded, "Our only chance of finding grounds for accusing Daniel will be in connection with the rules of his religion."

So the administrators and high officers went to the king and said, "Long live King Darius! We are all in agreement—we administrators, officials, high officers, advisers, and governors—that the king should make a law that will be strictly enforced. Give orders that for the next thirty days any person who prays to anyone, divine or human—except to you, Your Majesty—will be thrown into the den of lions. And now, Your Majesty, issue and sign this law so it cannot be changed, an official law of the Medes and Persians that cannot be revoked." So King Darius signed the law.

But when Daniel learned that the law had been signed, he went home and knelt down as usual in his upstairs room, with its windows open toward Jerusalem. He prayed three times a day, just as he had always done, giving thanks to his God.

Daniel 6:1–10 (NLT)

# Daniel in the Lions' Den

## Daniel 6

THE MEN WHO HAD SPOKEN to the king watched Daniel and saw him praying to his God for help. They went back to the king and said, "Didn't you make a law that forbids anyone to pray to any god or human except you for the next thirty days? And doesn't the law say that everyone who disobeys it will be thrown into a pit of lions?"

"Yes, that's the law I made," the king agreed. "And just like all written laws of the Medes and Persians, it cannot be changed."

The men then told the king, "That Jew named Daniel, who was brought here as a captive, refuses to obey you or the law that you ordered to be written. And he still prays to his god three times a day." The king was really upset to hear about this, and for the rest of the day he tried to think how he could save Daniel.

At sunset the men returned and said, "Your Majesty, remember that no written law of the Medes and Persians can be changed, not even by the king."

So Darius ordered Daniel to be brought out and thrown into a pit of lions. But he said to Daniel, "You have been faithful to your God, and I pray that he will rescue you."

At daybreak the king got up and ran to the pit. He was anxious and shouted, "Daniel, you were faithful and served your God. Was he able to save you from the lions?"

Daniel answered, "Your Majesty, I hope you live forever! My God knew that I was innocent, and he sent an angel to keep the lions from eating me."

The king was relieved to hear Daniel's voice, and he gave orders for him to be taken out of the pit. Daniel's faith in his God had kept him from being harmed.

Daniel 6:11–16, 19–23 (CEV)

# Rebuilding the Temple

## Ezra 1 and 3

IN THE FIRST YEAR OF KING CYRUS of Persia the LORD fulfilled the prophecy he had given through Jeremiah. He stirred the heart of Cyrus to put this proclamation in writing and to send it throughout his kingdom:

> "This is what King Cyrus of Persia says:
>
> "The LORD, the God of heaven, has given me all the kingdoms of the earth. He has appointed me to build him a Temple at Jerusalem, which is in Judah. Any of you who are his people may go to Jerusalem in Judah to rebuild this Temple of the LORD, the God of Israel, who lives in Jerusalem. And may your God be with you! Wherever this Jewish remnant is found, let their neighbors contribute toward their expenses by giving them silver and gold, supplies for the journey, and livestock, as well as a voluntary offering for the Temple of God in Jerusalem."

Then God stirred the hearts of the priests and Levites and the leaders of the tribes of Judah and Benjamin to go to Jerusalem to rebuild the Temple of the LORD.

When the builders completed the foundation of the LORD's Temple, the priests put on their robes and took their places to blow their trumpets. And the Levites, descendants of Asaph, clashed their cymbals to praise the LORD, just as King David had prescribed. With praise and thanks, they sang this song to the LORD:

> "He is so good!
> His faithful love for Israel endures forever!"

Then all the people gave a great shout, praising the LORD because the foundation of the LORD's Temple had been laid.

Ezra 1:1–5; 3:10–11 (NLT)

# Beautiful Queen Esther

## Esther 1 and 2

DURING THE THIRD YEAR of his rule, Xerxes gave a big dinner for all his officials and officers.

By the seventh day, King Xerxes was feeling happy because of so much wine. And he asked his seven personal servants to bring Queen Vashti to him.

The king's servants told Queen Vashti what he had said, but she refused to go to him, and this made him terribly angry.

After a while, King Xerxes got over being angry. But he kept thinking about what Vashti had done and the law that he had written because of her. Then the king's personal servants said:

> Your Majesty, a search must be made to find you some beautiful young women. Then let the young woman who pleases you most take Vashti's place as queen.

King Xerxes liked these suggestions, and he followed them.

At this time a Jew named Mordecai was living in Susa.

Mordecai had a very beautiful cousin named Esther, whose Hebrew name was Hadassah. He had raised her as his own daughter, after her father and mother died. When the king ordered the search for beautiful women, many were taken to the king's palace in Susa, and Esther was one of them.

Hegai was put in charge of all the women, and from the first day, Esther was his favorite. He began her beauty treatments at once. He also gave her plenty of food and seven special maids from the king's palace, and they had the best rooms.

Xerxes liked Esther more than he did any of the other young women. None of them pleased him as much as she did, and right away he fell in love with her and crowned her queen in place of Vashti.

Esther 1:3, 10–12; 2:1–2, 4–5, 7–9, 17 (CEV)

# Brave Queen Esther

## Esther 5 and 7

ESTHER PUT ON HER QUEEN'S CLOTHING and stood in the open space inside the king's special house in front of his throne room. The king was sitting on his throne in the throne room looking toward the door of his house. The king held his special golden stick in his hand toward Esther. So Esther came near and touched the top of the special stick. Then the king said to her, "What do you want, Queen Esther? What do you ask of me? You would be given even as much as half the nation." Esther said, "If it please the king, may the king and Haman come today to the special supper I have made ready for him."

So the king and Haman came to eat with Esther the queen. And the king said again to Esther on the second day, as they drank their wine at the special supper, "What do you want to ask of me, Queen Esther? It will be done for you. You would be given as much as half the nation." Queen Esther answered, "If I have found favor in your eyes, O king, and if it please the king, I ask that my life and the lives of my people be saved. For I and my people have been sold, to be destroyed, to be killed, and to be done away with. If we had only been sold as men and women servants, I would have kept quiet. For our trouble is not to be compared with the trouble it will make for the king." Then King Ahasuerus asked Queen Esther, "Who is he, and where is he, who would do such a thing?" Esther said, "This sinful Haman hates us very much!" Then Haman was very afraid in front of the king and queen. The king got up from drinking the wine very angry, and went into his garden, but Haman stayed to beg for his life from Queen Esther. He knew that the king planned to punish him.

Esther 5:1–4; 7:1–7 (NLV)

# Nehemiah Prays

## Nehemiah 1

THIS IS THE ACCOUNT of what Nehemiah son of Hacaliah accomplished.

In the month of Kislev in the twentieth year that Artaxerxes was emperor of Persia, I, Nehemiah, was in Susa, the capital city. Hanani, one of my brothers, arrived from Judah with another group, and I asked them about Jerusalem and about the other Jews who had returned from exile in Babylonia. They told me that those who had survived and were back in the homeland were in great difficulty and that the foreigners who lived nearby looked down on them. They also told me that the walls of Jerusalem were still broken down and that the gates had not been restored since the time they were burned. When I heard all this, I sat down and wept.

For several days I mourned and did not eat. I prayed to God, "LORD God of Heaven! You are great, and we stand in fear of you. You faithfully keep your covenant with those who love you and do what you command. Look at me, LORD, and hear my prayer, as I pray day and night for your servants, the people of Israel. I confess that we, the people of Israel, have sinned. My ancestors and I have sinned. We have acted wickedly against you and have not done what you commanded. We have not kept the laws which you gave us through Moses, your servant.

"Lord, these are your servants, your own people. You rescued them by your great power and strength. Listen now to my prayer and to the prayers of all your other servants who want to honor you. Give me success today and make the emperor merciful to me."

Nehemiah 1:1–7, 10–11 (GNT)

# Nehemiah's Prayer Answered

## Nehemiah 2

EARLY THE FOLLOWING SPRING, in the month of Nisan, during the twentieth year of King Artaxerxes' reign, I was serving the king his wine. I had never before appeared sad in his presence. So the king asked me, "Why are you looking so sad? You don't look sick to me. You must be deeply troubled."

Then I was terrified, but I replied, "Long live the king! How can I not be sad? For the city where my ancestors are buried is in ruins, and the gates have been destroyed by fire."

The king asked, "Well, how can I help you?"

With a prayer to the God of heaven, I replied, "If it please the king, and if you are pleased with me, your servant, send me to Judah to rebuild the city where my ancestors are buried."

The king, with the queen sitting beside him, asked, "How long will you be gone? When will you return?" After I told him how long I would be gone, the king agreed to my request.

I also said to the king, "If it please the king, let me have letters addressed to the governors of the province west of the Euphrates River, instructing them to let me travel safely through their territories on my way to Judah. And please give me a letter addressed to Asaph, the manager of the king's forest, instructing him to give me timber. I will need it to make beams for the gates of the Temple fortress, for the city walls, and for a house for myself." And the king granted these requests, because the gracious hand of God was on me.

Nehemiah 2:1–8 (NLT)

O.STEIN

# Nehemiah Rebuilds the Walls

## Nehemiah 2

SO I ARRIVED IN JERUSALEM. Three days later, I slipped out during the night, taking only a few others with me. I had not told anyone about the plans God had put in my heart for Jerusalem. We took no pack animals with us except the donkey I was riding. After dark I went out through the Valley Gate, past the Jackal's Well, and over to the Dung Gate to inspect the broken walls and burned gates. Then I went to the Fountain Gate and to the King's Pool, but my donkey couldn't get through the rubble. So, though it was still dark, I went up the Kidron Valley instead, inspecting the wall before I turned back and entered again at the Valley Gate.

The city officials did not know I had been out there or what I was doing, for I had not yet said anything to anyone about my plans. I had not yet spoken to the Jewish leaders—the priests, the nobles, the officials, or anyone else in the administration. But now I said to them, "You know very well what trouble we are in. Jerusalem lies in ruins, and its gates have been destroyed by fire. Let us rebuild the wall of Jerusalem and end this disgrace!" Then I told them about how the gracious hand of God had been on me, and about my conversation with the king.

They replied at once, "Yes, let's rebuild the wall!" So they began the good work.

Nehemiah 2:11–18 (NLT)

# Looking for the Savior

## Zechariah 9

REJOICE, REJOICE, people of Zion!
Shout for joy, you people of Jerusalem!
Look, your king is coming to you!
He comes triumphant and victorious,
but humble and riding on a donkey—
on a colt, the foal of a donkey.

The LORD says,
"I will remove the war chariots from Israel
and take the horses from Jerusalem;
the bows used in battle will be destroyed.
Your king will make peace among the nations;
he will rule from sea to sea,
from the Euphrates River to the ends of the earth."

The LORD says,
"Because of my covenant with you
that was sealed by the blood of sacrifices,
I will set your people free—
free from the waterless pit of exile.
When that day comes, the LORD will save his people,
as a shepherd saves his flock from danger.
They will shine in his land
like the jewels of a crown.
How good and beautiful the land will be!"

Zechariah 9:9–11, 16–17 (GNT)

# NEW TESTAMENT

# An Angel Appears to Zechariah

## Luke 1

WHEN HEROD WAS KING OF JUDEA, there was a Jewish priest named Zechariah. He was a member of the priestly order of Abijah, and his wife, Elizabeth, was also from the priestly line of Aaron. Zechariah and Elizabeth were righteous in God's eyes, careful to obey all of the Lord's commandments and regulations. They had no children because Elizabeth was unable to conceive, and they were both very old.

One day Zechariah was serving God in the Temple, for his order was on duty that week. As was the custom of the priests, he was chosen by lot to enter the sanctuary of the Lord and burn incense.

While Zechariah was in the sanctuary, an angel of the Lord appeared to him, standing to the right of the incense altar. Zechariah was shaken and overwhelmed with fear when he saw him. But the angel said, "Don't be afraid, Zechariah! God has heard your prayer. Your wife, Elizabeth, will give you a son, and you are to name him John.

"He will be a man with the spirit and power of Elijah. He will prepare the people for the coming of the Lord. He will turn the hearts of the fathers to their children, and he will cause those who are rebellious to accept the wisdom of the godly."

Zechariah said to the angel, "How can I be sure this will happen? I'm an old man now, and my wife is also well along in years."

Then the angel said, "I am Gabriel! I stand in the very presence of God. It was he who sent me to bring you this good news! But now, since you didn't believe what I said, you will be silent and unable to speak until the child is born. For my words will certainly be fulfilled at the proper time."

Luke 1:5–9, 11–13, 17–20 (NLT)

# An Angel Appears to Mary

## Luke 1

IN THE SIXTH MONTH of Elizabeth's pregnancy, God sent the angel Gabriel to Nazareth, a village in Galilee, to a virgin named Mary. She was engaged to be married to a man named Joseph, a descendant of King David. Gabriel appeared to her and said, "Greetings, favored woman! The Lord is with you!"

Confused and disturbed, Mary tried to think what the angel could mean. "Don't be afraid, Mary," the angel told her, "for you have found favor with God! You will conceive and give birth to a son, and you will name him Jesus. He will be very great and will be called the Son of the Most High. The Lord God will give him the throne of his ancestor David. And he will reign over Israel forever; his Kingdom will never end!"

Mary asked the angel, "But how can this happen? I am a virgin."

The angel replied, "The Holy Spirit will come upon you, and the power of the Most High will overshadow you. So the baby to be born will be holy, and he will be called the Son of God. What's more, your relative Elizabeth has become pregnant in her old age! People used to say she was barren, but she has conceived a son and is now in her sixth month. For the word of God will never fail."

Mary responded, "I am the Lord's servant. May everything you have said about me come true." And then the angel left her.

Luke 1:26–38 (NLT)

# Mary Visits Elizabeth

## Luke 1

A FEW DAYS LATER Mary hurried to the hill country of Judea, to the town where Zechariah lived. She entered the house and greeted Elizabeth. At the sound of Mary's greeting, Elizabeth's child leaped within her, and Elizabeth was filled with the Holy Spirit.

Elizabeth gave a glad cry and exclaimed to Mary, "God has blessed you above all women, and your child is blessed. Why am I so honored, that the mother of my Lord should visit me? When I heard your greeting, the baby in my womb jumped for joy. You are blessed because you believed that the Lord would do what he said."

### THE MAGNIFICAT: MARY'S SONG OF PRAISE

Mary responded,

"Oh, how my soul praises the Lord.
How my spirit rejoices in God my Savior!

For he took notice of his lowly servant girl,
and from now on all generations will call me blessed.

For the Mighty One is holy,
and he has done great things for me.

He shows mercy from generation to generation
to all who fear him.

His mighty arm has done tremendous things!
He has scattered the proud and haughty ones.

He has brought down princes from their thrones
and exalted the humble.

He has filled the hungry with good things
and sent the rich away with empty hands.

He has helped his servant Israel
and remembered to be merciful.

For he made this promise to our ancestors,
to Abraham and his children forever."

Luke 1:39–55 (NLT)

# John the Baptist Is Born

## Luke 1

WHEN THE TIME CAME, Elizabeth gave birth to a son. Her neighbors and family heard how the Lord had shown loving-kindness to her. They were happy for her. On the eighth day they did the religious act of the Jews on the child. They named him Zacharias [Zechariah], after his father. But his mother said, "No! His name is John." They said to her, "No one in your family has that name."

Then they talked to his father with their hands to find out what he would name the child. He asked for something to write on. He wrote, "His name is John." They were all surprised and wondered about it. Zacharias was able to talk from that time on and he gave thanks to God.

All those who lived near them were afraid. The news of what had happened was told through all the hill country of Judea. And all who heard those words remembered them and said, "What is this child going to be?" For the hand of the Lord was on him.

Luke 1:57–66 (NLV)

# Jesus Is Born

## Luke 2

AT THAT TIME THE ROMAN EMPEROR, Augustus, decreed that a census should be taken throughout the Roman Empire. (This was the first census taken when Quirinius was governor of Syria.) All returned to their own ancestral towns to register for this census. And because Joseph was a descendant of King David, he had to go to Bethlehem in Judea, David's ancient home. He traveled there from the village of Nazareth in Galilee. He took with him Mary, to whom he was engaged, who was now expecting a child.

And while they were there, the time came for her baby to be born. She gave birth to her firstborn son. She wrapped him snugly in strips of cloth and laid him in a manger, because there was no lodging available for them.

Luke 2:1–7 (NLT)

WOODWARD

# A Special Announcement

## Luke 2

THAT NIGHT THERE WERE SHEPHERDS staying in the fields nearby, guarding their flocks of sheep. Suddenly, an angel of the Lord appeared among them, and the radiance of the Lord's glory surrounded them. They were terrified, but the angel reassured them. "Don't be afraid!" he said. "I bring you good news that will bring great joy to all people. The Savior—yes, the Messiah, the Lord—has been born today in Bethlehem, the city of David! And you will recognize him by this sign: You will find a baby wrapped snugly in strips of cloth, lying in a manger."

Suddenly, the angel was joined by a vast host of others—the armies of heaven—praising God and saying,

"Glory to God in highest heaven,
and peace on earth to those with whom God is pleased."

Luke 2:8–14 (NLT)

# Shepherds Visit Jesus

## Luke 2

WHEN THE ANGELS had returned to heaven, the shepherds said to each other, "Let's go to Bethlehem! Let's see this thing that has happened, which the Lord has told us about."

They hurried to the village and found Mary and Joseph. And there was the baby, lying in the manger. After seeing him, the shepherds told everyone what had happened and what the angel had said to them about this child. All who heard the shepherds' story were astonished, but Mary kept all these things in her heart and thought about them often. The shepherds went back to their flocks, glorifying and praising God for all they had heard and seen. It was just as the angel had told them.

Luke 2:15–20 (NLT)

Zingaro

# Journey of the Wise Men

## Matthew 2

JESUS WAS BORN IN BETHLEHEM in Judea, during the reign of King Herod. About that time some wise men from eastern lands arrived in Jerusalem, asking, "Where is the newborn king of the Jews? We saw his star as it rose, and we have come to worship him."

King Herod was deeply disturbed when he heard this, as was everyone in Jerusalem. He called a meeting of the leading priests and teachers of religious law and asked, "Where is the Messiah supposed to be born?"

"In Bethlehem in Judea," they said, "for this is what the prophet wrote:

> 'And you, O Bethlehem in the land of Judah,
>     are not least among the ruling cities of Judah,
> for a ruler will come from you
>     who will be the shepherd for my people Israel.'"

Matthew 2:1–6 (NLT)

Rolfsen

# Jesus Presented in the Temple

## Luke 2

THE TIME CAME for Joseph and Mary to perform the ceremony of purification, as the Law of Moses commanded. So they took the child to Jerusalem to present him to the Lord, as it is written in the law of the Lord: "Every first-born male is to be dedicated to the Lord." They also went to offer a sacrifice of a pair of doves or two young pigeons, as required by the law of the Lord.

At that time there was a man named Simeon living in Jerusalem. He was a good, God-fearing man and was waiting for Israel to be saved. The Holy Spirit was with him and had assured him that he would not die before he had seen the Lord's promised Messiah. Led by the Spirit, Simeon went into the Temple. When the parents brought the child Jesus into the Temple to do for him what the Law required, Simeon took the child in his arms and gave thanks to God:

> "Now, Lord, you have kept your promise,
>     and you may let your servant go in peace.
> With my own eyes I have seen your salvation,
>     which you have prepared in the presence of all peoples:
> A light to reveal your will to the Gentiles
>     and bring glory to your people Israel."

The child's father and mother were amazed at the things Simeon said about him. Simeon blessed them and said to Mary, his mother, "This child is chosen by God for the destruction and the salvation of many in Israel. He will be a sign from God which many people will speak against and so reveal their secret thoughts. And sorrow, like a sharp sword, will break your own heart."

Luke 2:22–35 (GNT)

CLEVELAND
WOODWARD

# Visit of the Wise Men

## Matthew 2

THEN HEROD CALLED for a private meeting with the wise men, and he learned from them the time when the star first appeared. Then he told them, "Go to Bethlehem and search carefully for the child. And when you find him, come back and tell me so that I can go and worship him, too!"

After this interview the wise men went their way. And the star they had seen in the east guided them to Bethlehem. It went ahead of them and stopped over the place where the child was. When they saw the star, they were filled with joy! They entered the house and saw the child with his mother, Mary, and they bowed down and worshiped him. Then they opened their treasure chests and gave him gifts of gold, frankincense, and myrrh.

When it was time to leave, they returned to their own country by another route, for God had warned them in a dream not to return to Herod.

Matthew 2:7–12 (NLT)

# Escape to Egypt

## Matthew 2

AFTER THE WISE MEN were gone, an angel of the Lord appeared to Joseph in a dream. "Get up! Flee to Egypt with the child and his mother," the angel said. "Stay there until I tell you to return, because Herod is going to search for the child to kill him."

That night Joseph left for Egypt with the child and Mary, his mother, and they stayed there until Herod's death. This fulfilled what the Lord had spoken through the prophet: "I called my Son out of Egypt."

Herod was furious when he realized that the wise men had outwitted him.

Matthew 2:13–16 (NLT)

CLEVELAND
WOODWARD

# Joseph, Mary, and Jesus Move

## Matthew 2 and Luke 2

WHEN HEROD DIED, an angel of the Lord appeared in a dream to Joseph in Egypt. "Get up!" the angel said. "Take the child and his mother back to the land of Israel, because those who were trying to kill the child are dead."

So Joseph got up and returned to the land of Israel with Jesus and his mother. But when he learned that the new ruler of Judea was Herod's son Archelaus, he was afraid to go there. Then, after being warned in a dream, he left for the region of Galilee. So the family went and lived in a town called Nazareth. This fulfilled what the prophets had said: "He will be called a Nazarene."

Jesus grew in wisdom and in stature and in favor with God and all the people.

Matthew 2:19–23; Luke 2:52 (NLT)

H. Hofmann

# Mary Finds Jesus in the Temple

## Luke 2

EVERY YEAR JESUS' parents went to Jerusalem for the Passover festival. When Jesus was twelve years old, they attended the festival as usual. After the celebration was over, they started home to Nazareth, but Jesus stayed behind in Jerusalem. His parents didn't miss him at first, because they assumed he was among the other travelers. But when he didn't show up that evening, they started looking for him among their relatives and friends.

When they couldn't find him, they went back to Jerusalem to search for him there. Three days later they finally discovered him in the Temple, sitting among the religious teachers, listening to them and asking questions. All who heard him were amazed at his understanding and his answers.

His parents didn't know what to think. "Son," his mother said to him, "why have you done this to us? Your father and I have been frantic, searching for you everywhere."

"But why did you need to search?" he asked. "Didn't you know that I must be in my Father's house?" But they didn't understand what he meant.

Then he returned to Nazareth with them and was obedient to them. And his mother stored all these things in her heart.

Luke 2:41–51 (NLT)

# The Message of John the Baptist

## Mark 1

THE BEGINNING OF THE GOOD NEWS about Jesus the Messiah, the Son of God, as it is written in Isaiah the prophet:

"I will send my messenger ahead of you,
 who will prepare your way"—
"a voice of one calling in the wilderness,
'Prepare the way for the Lord,
 make straight paths for him.'"

And so John the Baptist appeared in the wilderness, preaching a baptism of repentance for the forgiveness of sins. The whole Judean countryside and all the people of Jerusalem went out to him. Confessing their sins, they were baptized by him in the Jordan River. John wore clothing made of camel's hair, with a leather belt around his waist, and he ate locusts and wild honey. And this was his message: "After me comes the one more powerful than I, the straps of whose sandals I am not worthy to stoop down and untie. I baptize you with water, but he will baptize you with the Holy Spirit."

Mark 1:1–8 (NIV)

# John Announces the Arrival of Jesus

## John 1

AND THIS IS THE TESTIMONY of John, when the Jews sent priests and Levites from Jerusalem to ask him, "Who are you?" He confessed, and did not deny, but confessed, "I am not the Christ." And they asked him, "What then? Are you Elijah?" He said, "I am not." "Are you the Prophet?" And he answered, "No." So they said to him, "Who are you? We need to give an answer to those who sent us. What do you say about yourself?" He said, "I am the voice of one crying out in the wilderness, 'Make straight the way of the Lord,' as the prophet Isaiah said."

They asked him, "Then why are you baptizing, if you are neither the Christ, nor Elijah, nor the Prophet?" John answered them, "I baptize with water, but among you stands one you do not know, even he who comes after me, the strap of whose sandal I am not worthy to untie."

The next day he saw Jesus coming toward him, and said, "Behold, the Lamb of God, who takes away the sin of the world! This is he of whom I said, 'After me comes a man who ranks before me, because he was before me.' I myself did not know him, but for this purpose I came baptizing with water, that he might be revealed to Israel."

John 1:19–23, 25–27, 29–31 (ESV)

# John Baptizes Jesus

## Matthew 3

THEN JESUS WENT FROM GALILEE to the Jordan River to be baptized by John. But John tried to talk him out of it. "I am the one who needs to be baptized by you," he said, "so why are you coming to me?"

But Jesus said, "It should be done, for we must carry out all that God requires." So John agreed to baptize him.

After his baptism, as Jesus came up out of the water, the heavens were opened and he saw the Spirit of God descending like a dove and settling on him. And a voice from heaven said, "This is my dearly loved Son, who brings me great joy."

Matthew 3:13–17 (NLT)

# John in Prison

## Matthew 11 and 14

WHEN JOHN THE BAPTIST heard in prison about the things that Christ was doing, he sent some of his disciples to him. "Tell us," they asked Jesus, "are you the one John said was going to come, or should we expect someone else?"

Jesus answered, "Go back and tell John what you are hearing and seeing: the blind can see, the lame can walk, those who suffer from dreaded skin diseases are made clean, the deaf hear, the dead are brought back to life, and the Good News is preached to the poor. How happy are those who have no doubts about me!"

While John's disciples were leaving, Jesus spoke about him to the crowds: "When you went out to John in the desert, what did you expect to see? A blade of grass bending in the wind? What did you go out to see? A man dressed up in fancy clothes? People who dress like that live in palaces! Tell me, what did you go out to see? A prophet? Yes indeed, but you saw much more than a prophet. For John is the one of whom the scripture says: 'God said, I will send my messenger ahead of you to open the way for you.' I assure you that John the Baptist is greater than anyone who has ever lived. But the one who is least in the Kingdom of heaven is greater than John."

At that time Herod, the ruler of Galilee, heard about Jesus. "He is really John the Baptist, who has come back to life," he told his officials. "That is why he has this power to perform miracles."

For Herod had earlier ordered John's arrest, and he had him tied up and put in prison. He had done this because of Herodias, his brother Philip's wife. For some time John the Baptist had told Herod, "It isn't right for you to be married to Herodias!" Herod wanted to kill him, but he was afraid of the Jewish people, because they considered John to be a prophet.

Matthew 11:2–11; 14:1–5 (GNT)

# Jesus Is Tempted by the Devil

## Matthew 4

THEN JESUS WAS LED BY THE SPIRIT into the wilderness to be tempted there by the devil. For forty days and forty nights he fasted and became very hungry.

During that time the devil came and said to him, "If you are the Son of God, tell these stones to become loaves of bread."

But Jesus told him, "No! The Scriptures say,

'People do not live by bread alone,
but by every word that comes from the mouth of God.'"

Then the devil took him to the holy city, Jerusalem, to the highest point of the Temple, and said, "If you are the Son of God, jump off! For the Scriptures say,

'He will order his angels to protect you.
And they will hold you up with their hands
so you won't even hurt your foot on a stone.'"

Jesus responded, "The Scriptures also say, 'You must not test the LORD your God.'"

Next the devil took him to the peak of a very high mountain and showed him all the kingdoms of the world and their glory. "I will give it all to you," he said, "if you will kneel down and worship me."

"Get out of here, Satan," Jesus told him. "For the Scriptures say,

'You must worship the LORD your God
and serve only him.'"

Then the devil went away, and angels came and took care of Jesus.

Matthew 4:1–11 (NLT)

Zingaro

# The Fishermen Follow Jesus

## Luke 5

ONE DAY AS JESUS was preaching on the shore of the Sea of Galilee, great crowds pressed in on him to listen to the word of God. He noticed two empty boats at the water's edge, for the fishermen had left them and were washing their nets. Stepping into one of the boats, Jesus asked Simon, its owner, to push it out into the water. So he sat in the boat and taught the crowds from there.

When he had finished speaking, he said to Simon, "Now go out where it is deeper, and let down your nets to catch some fish."

"Master," Simon replied, "we worked hard all last night and didn't catch a thing. But if you say so, I'll let the nets down again." And this time their nets were so full of fish they began to tear! A shout for help brought their partners in the other boat, and soon both boats were filled with fish and on the verge of sinking.

When Simon Peter realized what had happened, he fell to his knees before Jesus and said, "Oh, Lord, please leave me—I'm such a sinful man." For he was awestruck by the number of fish they had caught, as were the others with him. His partners, James and John, the sons of Zebedee, were also amazed.

Jesus replied to Simon, "Don't be afraid! From now on you'll be fishing for people!" And as soon as they landed, they left everything and followed Jesus.

Luke 5:1–11 (NLT)

# Matthew Meets Jesus

## Matthew 9

As JESUS WAS WALKING ALONG, he saw a man named Matthew sitting at his tax collector's booth. "Follow me and be my disciple," Jesus said to him. So Matthew got up and followed him.

Later, Matthew invited Jesus and his disciples to his home as dinner guests, along with many tax collectors and other disreputable sinners. But when the Pharisees saw this, they asked his disciples, "Why does your teacher eat with such scum?"

When Jesus heard this, he said, "Healthy people don't need a doctor—sick people do." Then he added, "Now go and learn the meaning of this Scripture: 'I want you to show mercy, not offer sacrifices.' For I have come to call not those who think they are righteous, but those who know they are sinners."

Matthew 9:9–13 (NLT)

# Jesus Chooses Twelve Disciples

## Luke 6

AT THAT TIME JESUS went up a hill to pray and spent the whole night there praying to God. When day came, he called his disciples to him and chose twelve of them, whom he named apostles: Simon (whom he named Peter) and his brother Andrew; James and John, Philip and Bartholomew, Matthew and Thomas, James son of Alphaeus, and Simon (who was called the Patriot), Judas son of James, and Judas Iscariot, who became the traitor.

### JESUS TEACHES AND HEALS

When Jesus had come down from the hill with the apostles, he stood on a level place with a large number of his disciples. A large crowd of people was there from all over Judea and from Jerusalem and from the coast cities of Tyre and Sidon; they had come to hear him and to be healed of their diseases. Those who were troubled by evil spirits also came and were healed. All the people tried to touch him, for power was going out from him and healing them all.

Luke 6:12–19 (GNT)

CLEVELAND
WOODWARD

# Jesus Performs His First Miracle

## John 2

THE NEXT DAY there was a wedding celebration in the village of Cana in Galilee. Jesus' mother was there, and Jesus and his disciples were also invited to the celebration. The wine supply ran out during the festivities, so Jesus' mother told him, "They have no more wine."

"Dear woman, that's not our problem," Jesus replied. "My time has not yet come."

But his mother told the servants, "Do whatever he tells you."

Standing nearby were six stone water jars, used for Jewish ceremonial washing. Each could hold twenty to thirty gallons. Jesus told the servants, "Fill the jars with water." When the jars had been filled, he said, "Now dip some out, and take it to the master of ceremonies." So the servants followed his instructions.

When the master of ceremonies tasted the water that was now wine, not knowing where it had come from (though, of course, the servants knew), he called the bridegroom over. "A host always serves the best wine first," he said. "Then, when everyone has had a lot to drink, he brings out the less expensive wine. But you have kept the best until now!"

This miraculous sign at Cana in Galilee was the first time Jesus revealed his glory. And his disciples believed in him.

John 2:1–11 (NLT)

# Jesus and Nicodemus

## John 3

NOW THERE WAS A MAN of the Pharisees named Nicodemus, a ruler of the Jews. This man came to Jesus by night and said to him, "Rabbi, we know that you are a teacher come from God, for no one can do these signs that you do unless God is with him." Jesus answered him, "Truly, truly, I say to you, unless one is born again he cannot see the kingdom of God." Nicodemus said to him, "How can a man be born when he is old? Can he enter a second time into his mother's womb and be born?" Jesus answered, "Truly, truly, I say to you, unless one is born of water and the Spirit, he cannot enter the kingdom of God. That which is born of the flesh is flesh, and that which is born of the Spirit is spirit. Do not marvel that I said to you, 'You must be born again.'"

Nicodemus said to him, "How can these things be?" Jesus answered him, "Are you the teacher of Israel and yet you do not understand these things? Truly, truly, I say to you, we speak of what we know, and bear witness to what we have seen, but you do not receive our testimony. If I have told you earthly things and you do not believe, how can you believe if I tell you heavenly things? No one has ascended into heaven except he who descended from heaven, the Son of Man. And as Moses lifted up the serpent in the wilderness, so must the Son of Man be lifted up, that whoever believes in him may have eternal life.

### FOR GOD SO LOVED THE WORLD

"For God so loved the world, that he gave his only Son, that whoever believes in him should not perish but have eternal life."

John 3:1–7, 9–16 (ESV)

# The Woman at the Well

## John 4

JESUS KNEW THE PHARISEES had heard that he was baptizing and making more disciples than John (though Jesus himself didn't baptize them—his disciples did). So he left Judea and returned to Galilee.

He had to go through Samaria on the way.

Soon a Samaritan woman came to draw water, and Jesus said to her, "Please give me a drink."

The woman was surprised, for Jews refuse to have anything to do with Samaritans. She said to Jesus, "You are a Jew, and I am a Samaritan woman. Why are you asking me for a drink?"

Jesus replied, "If you only knew the gift God has for you and who you are speaking to, you would ask me, and I would give you living water."

"But sir, you don't have a rope or a bucket," she said, "and this well is very deep. Where would you get this living water?"

Jesus replied, "Anyone who drinks this water will soon become thirsty again. But those who drink the water I give will never be thirsty again. It becomes a fresh, bubbling spring within them, giving them eternal life."

"Please, sir," the woman said, "give me this water! Then I'll never be thirsty again, and I won't have to come here to get water."

"Go and get your husband," Jesus told her.

"I don't have a husband," the woman replied.

Jesus said, "You're right! You don't have a husband—for you have had five husbands, and you aren't even married to the man you're living with now. You certainly spoke the truth!"

The woman said, "I know the Messiah is coming—the one who is called Christ. When he comes, he will explain everything to us."

Then Jesus told her, "I AM the Messiah!"

John 4:1–4, 7, 9–11, 13–18, 25–26 (NLT)

# Many Samaritans Believe

## John 4

THE WOMAN LEFT her water jar beside the well and ran back to the village, telling everyone, "Come and see a man who told me everything I ever did! Could he possibly be the Messiah?" So the people came streaming from the village to see him.

Many Samaritans from the village believed in Jesus because the woman had said, "He told me everything I ever did!" When they came out to see him, they begged him to stay in their village. So he stayed for two days, long enough for many more to hear his message and believe. Then they said to the woman, "Now we believe, not just because of what you told us, but because we have heard him ourselves. Now we know that he is indeed the Savior of the world."

John 4:28–30, 39–42 (NLT)

# Jesus Rejected in Nazareth

## Luke 4

WHEN HE CAME TO THE VILLAGE of Nazareth, his boyhood home, [Jesus] went as usual to the synagogue on the Sabbath and stood up to read the Scriptures. The scroll of Isaiah the prophet was handed to him.

"The Spirit of the LORD is upon me,
for he has anointed me to bring Good News to the poor.
He has sent me to proclaim that captives will be released,
that the blind will see,
that the oppressed will be set free,
and that the time of the LORD's favor has come."

He rolled up the scroll, handed it back to the attendant, and sat down. All eyes in the synagogue looked at him intently. Then he began to speak to them. "The Scripture you've just heard has been fulfilled this very day!"

Then he said, "You will undoubtedly quote me this proverb: 'Physician, heal yourself'—meaning, 'Do miracles here in your hometown like those you did in Capernaum.' But I tell you the truth, no prophet is accepted in his own hometown.

"Certainly there were many needy widows in Israel in Elijah's time, when the heavens were closed for three and a half years, and a severe famine devastated the land. Yet Elijah was not sent to any of them. He was sent instead to a foreigner—a widow of Zarephath in the land of Sidon. And many in Israel had leprosy in the time of the prophet Elisha, but the only one healed was Naaman, a Syrian."

When they heard this, the people in the synagogue were furious. Jumping up, they mobbed him and forced him to the edge of the hill on which the town was built. They intended to push him over the cliff, but he passed right through the crowd and went on his way.

Luke 4:16–21, 23–30 (NLT)

CLEVELAND
WOODWARD

# Jesus Heals Many People

## Luke 4

AFTER LEAVING THE SYNAGOGUE that day, Jesus went to Simon's home, where he found Simon's mother-in-law very sick with a high fever. "Please heal her," everyone begged. Standing at her bedside, he rebuked the fever, and it left her. And she got up at once and prepared a meal for them.

As the sun went down that evening, people throughout the village brought sick family members to Jesus. No matter what their diseases were, the touch of his hand healed every one. Many were possessed by demons; and the demons came out at his command, shouting, "You are the Son of God!" But because they knew he was the Messiah, he rebuked them and refused to let them speak.

### JESUS CONTINUES TO PREACH

Early the next morning Jesus went out to an isolated place. The crowds searched everywhere for him, and when they finally found him, they begged him not to leave them. But he replied, "I must preach the Good News of the Kingdom of God in other towns, too, because that is why I was sent." So he continued to travel around, preaching in synagogues throughout Judea.

Luke 4:38–44 (NLT)

CLEVELAND
WOODWARD

# Jesus Teaches the Beatitudes

## Matthew 5

SEEING THE CROWDS, he went up on the mountain, and when he sat down, his disciples came to him.

And he opened his mouth and taught them, saying:

Blessed are the poor in spirit, for theirs is the kingdom of heaven.

Blessed are those who mourn, for they shall be comforted.

Blessed are the meek, for they shall inherit the earth.

Blessed are those who hunger and thirst for righteousness,
for they shall be satisfied.

Blessed are the merciful, for they shall receive mercy.

Blessed are the pure in heart, for they shall see God.

Blessed are the peacemakers, for they shall be called sons of God.

Blessed are those who are persecuted for righteousness' sake,
for theirs is the kingdom of heaven.

Blessed are you when others revile you and persecute you and utter all kinds of evil against you falsely on my account. Rejoice and be glad, for your reward is great in heaven, for so they persecuted the prophets who were before you.

Matthew 5:1–12 (ESV)

H. Hofmann

# The Lord's Prayer

## Matthew 6

"And when you pray," [said Jesus,] "you must not be like the hypocrites. For they love to stand and pray in the synagogues and at the street corners, that they may be seen by others. Truly, I say to you, they have received their reward. But when you pray, go into your room and shut the door and pray to your Father who is in secret. And your Father who sees in secret will reward you.

"And when you pray, do not heap up empty phrases as the Gentiles do, for they think that they will be heard for their many words. Do not be like them, for your Father knows what you need before you ask him. Pray then like this: . . .

Matthew 6:5–9 (ESV)

# The Lord's Prayer

Our Father which art in heaven, Hallowed be thy name. Thy kingdom come. Thy will be done in earth, as it is in heaven.

Give us this day our daily bread. And forgive us our debts as we forgive our debtors. And lead us not into temptation, but deliver us from evil: For thine is the kingdom, and the power, and the glory, forever.

Amen.

# God Cares for You

## Matthew 6

"DON'T STORE UP TREASURES here on earth," [said Jesus,] "where moths eat them and rust destroys them, and where thieves break in and steal. Store your treasures in heaven, where moths and rust cannot destroy, and thieves do not break in and steal. Wherever your treasure is, there the desires of your heart will also be."

"No one can serve two masters. For you will hate one and love the other; you will be devoted to one and despise the other. You cannot serve God and be enslaved to money.

"That is why I tell you not to worry about everyday life—whether you have enough food and drink, or enough clothes to wear. Isn't life more than food, and your body more than clothing? Look at the birds. They don't plant or harvest or store food in barns, for your heavenly Father feeds them. And aren't you far more valuable to him than they are? Can all your worries add a single moment to your life?

"And why worry about your clothing? Look at the lilies of the field and how they grow. They don't work or make their clothing, yet Solomon in all his glory was not dressed as beautifully as they are. And if God cares so wonderfully for wildflowers that are here today and thrown into the fire tomorrow, he will certainly care for you. Why do you have so little faith?

"So don't worry about these things, saying, 'What will we eat? What will we drink? What will we wear?' These things dominate the thoughts of unbelievers, but your heavenly Father already knows all your needs. Seek the Kingdom of God above all else, and live righteously, and he will give you everything you need."

Matthew 6:19–21, 24–33 (NLT)

# The Wise and Foolish Builders

## Matthew 5 and 7

JESUS WENT UP ON THE MOUNTAINSIDE and sat down. His disciples gathered around him, and he began to teach them.

"Anyone who listens to my teaching and follows it is wise, like a person who builds a house on solid rock. Though the rain comes in torrents and the floodwaters rise and the winds beat against that house, it won't collapse because it is built on bedrock. But anyone who hears my teaching and doesn't obey it is foolish, like a person who builds a house on sand. When the rains and floods come and the winds beat against that house, it will collapse with a mighty crash."

When Jesus had finished saying these things, the crowds were amazed at his teaching, for he taught with real authority—quite unlike their teachers of religious law.

Matthew 5:1–2; 7:24–29 (NLT)

# Jesus Sends Seventy-Two Disciples

## Luke 10

AFTER THIS THE LORD appointed seventy-two others and sent them on ahead of him, two by two, into every town and place where he himself was about to go. And he said to them, "The harvest is plentiful, but the laborers are few. Therefore pray earnestly to the Lord of the harvest to send out laborers into his harvest. Go your way; behold, I am sending you out as lambs in the midst of wolves. Carry no moneybag, no knapsack, no sandals, and greet no one on the road. Whatever house you enter, first say, 'Peace be to this house!' And if a son of peace is there, your peace will rest upon him. But if not, it will return to you. And remain in the same house, eating and drinking what they provide, for the laborer deserves his wages. Do not go from house to house. Whenever you enter a town and they receive you, eat what is set before you. Heal the sick in it and say to them, 'The kingdom of God has come near to you.' But whenever you enter a town and they do not receive you, go into its streets and say, 'Even the dust of your town that clings to our feet we wipe off against you. Nevertheless know this, that the kingdom of God has come near.' I tell you, it will be more bearable on that day for Sodom than for that town.

"The one who hears you hears me, and the one who rejects you rejects me, and the one who rejects me rejects him who sent me."

The seventy-two returned with joy, saying, "Lord, even the demons are subject to us in your name!"

Luke 10:1–12, 16–17 (ESV)

O. Stemler.

# Jesus' Parable of the Good Samaritan

## Luke 10

AND BEHOLD, a lawyer stood up to put [Jesus] to the test, saying, "Teacher, what shall I do to inherit eternal life?" [Jesus] said to him, "What is written in the Law? How do you read it?" And he answered, "You shall love the Lord your God with all your heart and with all your soul and with all your strength and with all your mind, and your neighbor as yourself." And [Jesus] said to him, "You have answered correctly; do this, and you will live."

But he, desiring to justify himself, said to Jesus, "And who is my neighbor?" Jesus replied, "A man was going down from Jerusalem to Jericho, and he fell among robbers, who stripped him and beat him and departed, leaving him half dead. Now by chance a priest was going down that road, and when he saw him he passed by on the other side. So likewise a Levite, when he came to the place and saw him, passed by on the other side. But a Samaritan, as he journeyed, came to where he was, and when he saw him, he had compassion. He went to him and bound up his wounds, pouring on oil and wine. Then he set him on his own animal and brought him to an inn and took care of him. And the next day he took out two denarii and gave them to the innkeeper, saying, 'Take care of him, and whatever more you spend, I will repay you when I come back.' Which of these three, do you think, proved to be a neighbor to the man who fell among the robbers?" He said, "The one who showed him mercy." And Jesus said to him, "You go, and do likewise."

Luke 10:25–37 (ESV)

lockhorst

# Jesus Visits Martha and Mary

## Luke 10

AS JESUS AND THE DISCIPLES continued on their way to Jerusalem, they came to a certain village where a woman named Martha welcomed him into her home. Her sister, Mary, sat at the Lord's feet, listening to what he taught. But Martha was distracted by the big dinner she was preparing. She came to Jesus and said, "Lord, doesn't it seem unfair to you that my sister just sits here while I do all the work? Tell her to come and help me."

But the Lord said to her, "My dear Martha, you are worried and upset over all these details! There is only one thing worth being concerned about. Mary has discovered it, and it will not be taken away from her."

Luke 10:38–42 (NLT)

# The Midnight Visitor

## Luke 11

AND JESUS SAID TO HIS DISCIPLES, "Suppose one of you should go to a friend's house at midnight and say, 'Friend, let me borrow three loaves of bread. A friend of mine who is on a trip has just come to my house, and I don't have any food for him!' And suppose your friend should answer from inside, 'Don't bother me! The door is already locked, and my children and I are in bed. I can't get up and give you anything.' Well, what then? I tell you that even if he will not get up and give you the bread because you are his friend, yet he will get up and give you everything you need because you are not ashamed to keep on asking. And so I say to you: Ask, and you will receive; seek, and you will find; knock, and the door will be opened to you. For those who ask will receive, and those who seek will find, and the door will be opened to anyone who knocks. Would any of you who are fathers give your son a snake when he asks for fish? Or would you give him a scorpion when he asks for an egg? As bad as you are, you know how to give good things to your children. How much more, then, will the Father in heaven give the Holy Spirit to those who ask him!"

Luke 11:5–13 (GNT)

# The Parable of the Rich Fool

## Luke 12

THEN SOMEONE CALLED from the crowd, "Teacher, please tell my brother to divide our father's estate with me."

Jesus replied, "Friend, who made me a judge over you to decide such things as that?" Then he said, "Beware! Guard against every kind of greed. Life is not measured by how much you own."

Then he told them a story: "A rich man had a fertile farm that produced fine crops. He said to himself, 'What should I do? I don't have room for all my crops.' Then he said, 'I know! I'll tear down my barns and build bigger ones. Then I'll have room enough to store all my wheat and other goods. And I'll sit back and say to myself, "My friend, you have enough stored away for years to come. Now take it easy! Eat, drink, and be merry!"'

"But God said to him, 'You fool! You will die this very night. Then who will get everything you worked for?'

"Yes, a person is a fool to store up earthly wealth but not have a rich relationship with God."

Luke 12:13–21 (NLT)

# A Question About the Sabbath

## Matthew 12

ONE SABBATH, Jesus and his disciples were walking through some wheat fields. His disciples were hungry and began picking and eating grains of wheat. Some Pharisees noticed this and said to Jesus, "Why are your disciples picking grain on the Sabbath? They are not supposed to do that!"

Jesus answered:

> You surely must have read what David did when he and his followers were hungry. He went into the house of God, and then they ate the sacred loaves of bread that only priests are supposed to eat. Haven't you read in the Law of Moses that the priests are allowed to work in the temple on the Sabbath? But no one says that they are guilty of breaking the law of the Sabbath. I tell you that there is something here greater than the temple. Don't you know what the Scriptures mean when they say, "Instead of offering sacrifices to me, I want you to be merciful to others?" If you knew what this means, you would not condemn these innocent disciples of mine. So the Son of Man is Lord over the Sabbath.

Matthew 12:1–8 (CEV)

# A Farmer Plants Seeds

## Matthew 13

LATER THAT SAME DAY JESUS left the house and sat beside the lake. He told many stories in the form of parables, such as this one:

"Listen! A farmer went out to plant some seeds. As he scattered them across his field, some seeds fell on a footpath, and the birds came and ate them. Other seeds fell on shallow soil with underlying rock. The seeds sprouted quickly because the soil was shallow. But the plants soon wilted under the hot sun, and since they didn't have deep roots, they died. Other seeds fell among thorns that grew up and choked out the tender plants. Still other seeds fell on fertile soil, and they produced a crop that was thirty, sixty, and even a hundred times as much as had been planted! Anyone with ears to hear should listen and understand.

"Now listen to the explanation of the parable about the farmer planting seeds: The seed that fell on the footpath represents those who hear the message about the Kingdom and don't understand it. Then the evil one comes and snatches away the seed that was planted in their hearts. The seed on the rocky soil represents those who hear the message and immediately receive it with joy. But since they don't have deep roots, they don't last long. They fall away as soon as they have problems or are persecuted for believing God's word. The seed that fell among the thorns represents those who hear God's word, but all too quickly the message is crowded out by the worries of this life and the lure of wealth, so no fruit is produced. The seed that fell on good soil represents those who truly hear and understand God's word and produce a harvest of thirty, sixty, or even a hundred times as much as had been planted!"

Matthew 13:1, 3–9, 18–23 (NLT)

# The Parable of the Wheat and Weeds

## Matthew 13

HERE IS ANOTHER STORY Jesus told: "The Kingdom of Heaven is like a farmer who planted good seed in his field. But that night as the workers slept, his enemy came and planted weeds among the wheat, then slipped away. When the crop began to grow and produce grain, the weeds also grew.

"The farmer's workers went to him and said, 'Sir, the field where you planted that good seed is full of weeds! Where did they come from?'

"'An enemy has done this!' the farmer exclaimed.

"'Should we pull out the weeds?' they asked.

"'No,' he replied, 'you'll uproot the wheat if you do. Let both grow together until the harvest. Then I will tell the harvesters to sort out the weeds, tie them into bundles, and burn them, and to put the wheat in the barn.'"

Then, leaving the crowds outside, Jesus went into the house. His disciples said, "Please explain to us the story of the weeds in the field."

Jesus replied, "The Son of Man is the farmer who plants the good seed. The field is the world, and the good seed represents the people of the Kingdom. The weeds are the people who belong to the evil one. The enemy who planted the weeds among the wheat is the devil. The harvest is the end of the world, and the harvesters are the angels.

"Just as the weeds are sorted out and burned in the fire, so it will be at the end of the world. The Son of Man will send his angels, and they will remove from his Kingdom everything that causes sin and all who do evil."

Matthew 13:24–30, 36–41 (NLT)

# Jesus Corrects the Pharisees

## Matthew 15

THEN PHARISEES AND SCRIBES came to Jesus from Jerusalem and said, "Why do your disciples break the tradition of the elders? For they do not wash their hands when they eat." He answered them, "And why do you break the commandment of God for the sake of your tradition? For God commanded, 'Honor your father and your mother,' and, 'Whoever reviles father or mother must surely die.' But you say, 'If anyone tells his father or his mother, "What you would have gained from me is given to God," he need not honor his father.' So for the sake of your tradition you have made void the word of God. You hypocrites! Well did Isaiah prophesy of you, when he said:

"'This people honors me with their lips,
　　but their heart is far from me;
in vain do they worship me,
　　teaching as doctrines the commandments of men.'"

And he called the people to him and said to them, "Hear and understand: it is not what goes into the mouth that defiles a person, but what comes out of the mouth; this defiles a person." Then the disciples came and said to him, "Do you know that the Pharisees were offended when they heard this saying?" He answered, "Every plant that my heavenly Father has not planted will be rooted up. Let them alone; they are blind guides. And if the blind lead the blind, both will fall into a pit." But Peter said to him, "Explain the parable to us." And he said, "Are you also still without understanding? Do you not see that whatever goes into the mouth passes into the stomach and is expelled? But what comes out of the mouth proceeds from the heart, and this defiles a person."

Matthew 15:1–18 (ESV)

# The Parable of the Banquet

## Luke 14

THEN JESUS SAID to the leader of the proud religious law-keepers, "There was a man who was giving a big supper. He asked many people to come to eat. When it was about time to eat, he sent one of the servants he owned to tell those he had asked, saying, 'Come, everything is ready now.' They all gave different reasons why they could not come. The first said, 'I have bought some land and I must go and see it. Do not expect me to come.' Another one said, 'I have bought ten cows to use for working in my fields. I must go and try them out. Do not expect me to come.' And another one said, 'I have just been married and I cannot come.'

"The servant went back to his owner and told him these things. Then his owner became angry. He said to his servant, 'Hurry into the streets and narrow roads of the city and bring poor people here. Bring those whose bodies are diseased. Bring those who cannot walk and those who are blind.' The servant came back and said, 'Sir, what you told me to do has been done. But there are still some empty places.' Then the owner said to his servant, 'Go out along the roads leading away from the city and into the fields. Tell them they must come. Do this so my house will be filled. I tell you, not one of those I had asked will eat of my supper.'"

Luke 14:16–24 (NLV)

# The Parable of the Prodigal Son

## Luke 15

"THERE WAS A MAN WHO HAD TWO SONS," [said Jesus.] "And the younger of them said to his father, 'Father, give me the share of property that is coming to me.' And he divided his property between them. Not many days later, the younger son gathered all he had and took a journey into a far country, and there he squandered his property in reckless living. And when he had spent everything, a severe famine arose in that country, and he began to be in need. So he went and hired himself out to one of the citizens of that country, who sent him into his fields to feed pigs. And he was longing to be fed with the pods that the pigs ate, and no one gave him anything.

"But when he came to himself, he said, 'How many of my father's hired servants have more than enough bread, but I perish here with hunger! I will arise and go to my father, and I will say to him, "Father, I have sinned against heaven and before you. I am no longer worthy to be called your son. Treat me as one of your hired servants."' And he arose and came to his father. But while he was still a long way off, his father saw him and felt compassion, and ran and embraced him and kissed him. And the son said to him, 'Father, I have sinned against heaven and before you. I am no longer worthy to be called your son.' But the father said to his servants, 'Bring quickly the best robe, and put it on him, and put a ring on his hand, and shoes on his feet. And bring the fattened calf and kill it, and let us eat and celebrate. For this my son was dead, and is alive again; he was lost, and is found.'"

Luke 15:11–24 (ESV)

# Parable of the Rich Man and Poor Man

## Luke 16

JESUS SAID, "There was a certain rich man who was splendidly clothed in purple and fine linen and who lived each day in luxury. At his gate lay a poor man named Lazarus who was covered with sores. As Lazarus lay there longing for scraps from the rich man's table, the dogs would come and lick his open sores.

"Finally, the poor man died and was carried by the angels to sit beside Abraham at the heavenly banquet. The rich man also died and was buried, and he went to the place of the dead. There, in torment, he saw Abraham in the far distance with Lazarus at his side.

"The rich man shouted, 'Father Abraham, have some pity! Send Lazarus over here to dip the tip of his finger in water and cool my tongue. I am in anguish in these flames.'

"But Abraham said to him, 'Son, remember that during your lifetime you had everything you wanted, and Lazarus had nothing. So now he is here being comforted, and you are in anguish. And besides, there is a great chasm separating us. No one can cross over to you from here, and no one can cross over to us from there.'

"Then the rich man said, 'Please, Father Abraham, at least send him to my father's home. For I have five brothers, and I want him to warn them so they don't end up in this place of torment.'

"But Abraham said, 'Moses and the prophets have warned them. Your brothers can read what they wrote.'

"The rich man replied, 'No, Father Abraham! But if someone is sent to them from the dead, then they will repent of their sins and turn to God.'

"But Abraham said, 'If they won't listen to Moses and the prophets, they won't be persuaded even if someone rises from the dead.'"

Luke 16:19–31 (NLT)

# The Persistent Widow

## Luke 18

ONE DAY JESUS told his disciples a story to show that they should always pray and never give up. "There was a judge in a certain city," he said, "who neither feared God nor cared about people. A widow of that city came to him repeatedly, saying, 'Give me justice in this dispute with my enemy.' The judge ignored her for a while, but finally he said to himself, 'I don't fear God or care about people, but this woman is driving me crazy. I'm going to see that she gets justice, because she is wearing me out with her constant requests!'"

Then the Lord said, "Learn a lesson from this unjust judge. Even he rendered a just decision in the end. So don't you think God will surely give justice to his chosen people who cry out to him day and night? Will he keep putting them off? I tell you, he will grant justice to them quickly! But when the Son of Man returns, how many will he find on the earth who have faith?"

Luke 18:1–8 (NLT)

# The Pharisee and Tax Collector

## Luke 18

THEN JESUS TOLD THIS STORY to some who had great confidence in their own righteousness and scorned everyone else: "Two men went to the Temple to pray. One was a Pharisee, and the other was a despised tax collector. The Pharisee stood by himself and prayed this prayer: 'I thank you, God, that I am not like other people—cheaters, sinners, adulterers. I'm certainly not like that tax collector! I fast twice a week, and I give you a tenth of my income.'

"But the tax collector stood at a distance and dared not even lift his eyes to heaven as he prayed. Instead, he beat his chest in sorrow, saying, 'O God, be merciful to me, for I am a sinner.' I tell you, this sinner, not the Pharisee, returned home justified before God. For those who exalt themselves will be humbled, and those who humble themselves will be exalted."

Luke 18:9–14 (NLT)

# Jesus Welcomes Children

## Matthew 18 and 19

ABOUT THAT TIME the disciples came to Jesus and asked, "Who is greatest in the Kingdom of Heaven?"

Jesus called a little child to him and put the child among them. Then he said, "I tell you the truth, unless you turn from your sins and become like little children, you will never get into the Kingdom of Heaven. So anyone who becomes as humble as this little child is the greatest in the Kingdom of Heaven.

"And anyone who welcomes a little child like this on my behalf is welcoming me."

### JESUS BLESSES THE CHILDREN

One day some parents brought their children to Jesus so he could lay his hands on them and pray for them. But the disciples scolded the parents for bothering him.

But Jesus said, "Let the children come to me. Don't stop them! For the Kingdom of Heaven belongs to those who are like these children." And he placed his hands on their heads and blessed them before he left.

Matthew 18:1–5; 19:13–15 (NLT)

CLEVELAND
WOODWARD

# Zacchaeus Meets Jesus

## Luke 19

JESUS ENTERED JERICHO and made his way through the town. There was a man there named Zacchaeus. He was the chief tax collector in the region, and he had become very rich. He tried to get a look at Jesus, but he was too short to see over the crowd. So he ran ahead and climbed a sycamore-fig tree beside the road, for Jesus was going to pass that way.

When Jesus came by, he looked up at Zacchaeus and called him by name. "Zacchaeus!" he said. "Quick, come down! I must be a guest in your home today."

Zacchaeus quickly climbed down and took Jesus to his house in great excitement and joy. But the people were displeased. "He has gone to be the guest of a notorious sinner," they grumbled.

Meanwhile, Zacchaeus stood before the Lord and said, "I will give half my wealth to the poor, Lord, and if I have cheated people on their taxes, I will give them back four times as much!"

Jesus responded, "Salvation has come to this home today, for this man has shown himself to be a true son of Abraham. For the Son of Man came to seek and save those who are lost."

Luke 19:1–10 (NLT)

# Jesus and a Rich Young Man

## Mark 10

AS JESUS WAS STARTING OUT on his way to Jerusalem, a man came running up to him, knelt down, and asked, "Good Teacher, what must I do to inherit eternal life?"

"Why do you call me good?" Jesus asked. "Only God is truly good. But to answer your question, you know the commandments: 'You must not murder. You must not commit adultery. You must not steal. You must not testify falsely. You must not cheat anyone. Honor your father and mother.'"

"Teacher," the man replied, "I've obeyed all these commandments since I was young."

Looking at the man, Jesus felt genuine love for him. "There is still one thing you haven't done," he told him. "Go and sell all your possessions and give the money to the poor, and you will have treasure in heaven. Then come, follow me."

At this the man's face fell, and he went away sad, for he had many possessions.

Jesus looked around and said to his disciples, "How hard it is for the rich to enter the Kingdom of God!" This amazed them. But Jesus said again, "Dear children, it is very hard to enter the Kingdom of God. In fact, it is easier for a camel to go through the eye of a needle than for a rich person to enter the Kingdom of God!"

The disciples were astounded. "Then who in the world can be saved?" they asked.

Jesus looked at them intently and said, "Humanly speaking, it is impossible. But not with God. Everything is possible with God."

Mark 10:17–27 (NLT)

CLEVELAND
WOODWARD

# The Parable of the Workers

## Matthew 20

"FOR THE KINGDOM OF HEAVEN is like a master of a house who went out early in the morning to hire laborers for his vineyard," [Jesus said.] "After agreeing with the laborers for a denarius a day, he sent them into his vineyard. And going out about the third hour he saw others standing idle in the marketplace, and to them he said, 'You go into the vineyard too, and whatever is right I will give you.' So they went. Going out again about the sixth hour and the ninth hour, he did the same. And about the eleventh hour he went out and found others standing. And he said to them, 'Why do you stand here idle all day?' They said to him, 'Because no one has hired us.' He said to them, 'You go into the vineyard too.' And when evening came, the owner of the vineyard said to his foreman, 'Call the laborers and pay them their wages, beginning with the last, up to the first.' And when those hired about the eleventh hour came, each of them received a denarius. Now when those hired first came, they thought they would receive more, but each of them also received a denarius. And on receiving it they grumbled at the master of the house, saying, 'These last worked only one hour, and you have made them equal to us who have borne the burden of the day and the scorching heat.' But he replied to one of them, 'Friend, I am doing you no wrong. Did you not agree with me for a denarius? I choose to give to this last worker as I give to you. Am I not allowed to do what I choose with what belongs to me? Or do you begrudge my generosity?' So the last will be first, and the first last."

Matthew 20:1–16 (ESV)

# The Pharisees Try to Trick Jesus

## Matthew 22

THEN THE PHARISEES went and plotted how to entangle [Jesus] in his words. And they sent their disciples to him, along with the Herodians, saying, "Teacher, we know that you are true and teach the way of God truthfully, and you do not care about anyone's opinion, for you are not swayed by appearances. Tell us, then, what you think. Is it lawful to pay taxes to Caesar, or not?" But Jesus, aware of their malice, said, "Why put me to the test, you hypocrites? Show me the coin for the tax." And they brought him a denarius. And Jesus said to them, "Whose likeness and inscription is this?" They said, "Caesar's." Then he said to them, "Therefore render to Caesar the things that are Caesar's, and to God the things that are God's." When they heard it, they marveled. And they left him and went away.

Matthew 22:15–22 (ESV)

# Jesus Teaches About Generous Giving

## Mark 12

JESUS ALSO TAUGHT: "Beware of these teachers of religious law! For they like to parade around in flowing robes and receive respectful greetings as they walk in the marketplaces. And how they love the seats of honor in the synagogues and the head table at banquets. Yet they shamelessly cheat widows out of their property and then pretend to be pious by making long prayers in public. Because of this, they will be more severely punished."

### THE WIDOW'S OFFERING

Jesus sat down near the collection box in the Temple and watched as the crowds dropped in their money. Many rich people put in large amounts. Then a poor widow came and dropped in two small coins.

Jesus called his disciples to him and said, "I tell you the truth, this poor widow has given more than all the others who are making contributions. For they gave a tiny part of their surplus, but she, poor as she is, has given everything she had to live on."

Mark 12:38–44 (NLT)

# Signs of a True Jesus Follower

## Matthew 25

"WHEN THE SON OF MAN comes in his glory, and all the angels with him, then he will sit on his glorious throne. Before him will be gathered all the nations, and he will separate people one from another as a shepherd separates the sheep from the goats. And he will place the sheep on his right, but the goats on the left. Then the King will say to those on his right, 'Come, you who are blessed by my Father, inherit the kingdom prepared for you from the foundation of the world. For I was hungry and you gave me food, I was thirsty and you gave me drink, I was a stranger and you welcomed me, I was naked and you clothed me, I was sick and you visited me, I was in prison and you came to me.' Then the righteous will answer him, saying, 'Lord, when did we see you hungry and feed you, or thirsty and give you drink? And when did we see you a stranger and welcome you, or naked and clothe you? And when did we see you sick or in prison and visit you?' And the King will answer them, 'Truly, I say to you, as you did it to one of the least of these my brothers, you did it to me.'"

Matthew 25:31–40 (ESV)

# Jesus Heals a Dying Boy

## John 4

JESUS WENT ON TO GALILEE.

As he traveled through Galilee, he came to Cana, where he had turned the water into wine. There was a government official in nearby Capernaum whose son was very sick. When he heard that Jesus had come from Judea to Galilee, he went and begged Jesus to come to Capernaum to heal his son, who was about to die.

Jesus asked, "Will you never believe in me unless you see miraculous signs and wonders?"

The official pleaded, "Lord, please come now before my little boy dies."

Then Jesus told him, "Go back home. Your son will live!" And the man believed what Jesus said and started home.

While the man was on his way, some of his servants met him with the news that his son was alive and well. He asked them when the boy had begun to get better, and they replied, "Yesterday afternoon at one o'clock his fever suddenly disappeared!" Then the father realized that that was the very time Jesus had told him, "Your son will live." And he and his entire household believed in Jesus. This was the second miraculous sign Jesus did in Galilee after coming from Judea.

John 4:43, 46–54 (NLT)

# Healing at the Pool of Bethesda

## John 5

THERE WAS A FEAST OF THE JEWS, and Jesus went up to Jerusalem.

Now there is in Jerusalem by the Sheep Gate a pool, in Aramaic called Bethesda, which has five roofed colonnades. In these lay a multitude of invalids—blind, lame, and paralyzed. One man was there who had been an invalid for thirty-eight years. When Jesus saw him lying there and knew that he had already been there a long time, he said to him, "Do you want to be healed?" The sick man answered him, "Sir, I have no one to put me into the pool when the water is stirred up, and while I am going another steps down before me." Jesus said to him, "Get up, take up your bed, and walk." And at once the man was healed, and he took up his bed and walked.

John 5:1–9 (ESV)

# Jesus Heals a Paralyzed Man

## Mark 2

When Jesus returned to Capernaum several days later, the news spread quickly that he was back home. Soon the house where he was staying was so packed with visitors that there was no more room, even outside the door. While he was preaching God's word to them, four men arrived carrying a paralyzed man on a mat. They couldn't bring him to Jesus because of the crowd, so they dug a hole through the roof above his head. Then they lowered the man on his mat, right down in front of Jesus. Seeing their faith, Jesus said to the paralyzed man, "My child, your sins are forgiven."

But some of the teachers of religious law who were sitting there thought to themselves, "What is he saying? This is blasphemy! Only God can forgive sins!"

Jesus knew immediately what they were thinking, so he asked them, "Why do you question this in your hearts? Is it easier to say to the paralyzed man 'Your sins are forgiven,' or 'Stand up, pick up your mat, and walk'? So I will prove to you that the Son of Man has the authority on earth to forgive sins." Then Jesus turned to the paralyzed man and said, "Stand up, pick up your mat, and go home!"

And the man jumped up, grabbed his mat, and walked out through the stunned onlookers. They were all amazed and praised God, exclaiming, "We've never seen anything like this before!"

Mark 2:1–12 (NLT)

# Jesus Heals on the Sabbath

## Luke 6

ON ANOTHER SABBATH DAY, a man with a deformed right hand was in the synagogue while Jesus was teaching. The teachers of religious law and the Pharisees watched Jesus closely. If he healed the man's hand, they planned to accuse him of working on the Sabbath.

But Jesus knew their thoughts. He said to the man with the deformed hand, "Come and stand in front of everyone." So the man came forward. Then Jesus said to his critics, "I have a question for you. Does the law permit good deeds on the Sabbath, or is it a day for doing evil? Is this a day to save life or to destroy it?"

He looked around at them one by one and then said to the man, "Hold out your hand." So the man held out his hand, and it was restored! At this, the enemies of Jesus were wild with rage and began to discuss what to do with him.

Luke 6:6–11 (NLT)

# Jesus Heals a Centurion's Servant

## Matthew 8

WHEN [JESUS] HAD ENTERED CAPERNAUM, a centurion came forward to him, appealing to him, "Lord, my servant is lying paralyzed at home, suffering terribly." And he said to him, "I will come and heal him." But the centurion replied, "Lord, I am not worthy to have you come under my roof, but only say the word, and my servant will be healed. For I too am a man under authority, with soldiers under me. And I say to one, 'Go,' and he goes, and to another, 'Come,' and he comes, and to my servant, 'Do this,' and he does it." When Jesus heard this, he marveled and said to those who followed him, "Truly, I tell you, with no one in Israel have I found such faith." And to the centurion Jesus said, "Go; let it be done for you as you have believed." And the servant was healed at that very moment.

Matthew 8:5–10, 13 (ESV)

# Jesus Calms a Storm

## Mark 4

AS EVENING CAME, Jesus said to his disciples, "Let's cross to the other side of the lake." So they took Jesus in the boat and started out, leaving the crowds behind (although other boats followed). But soon a fierce storm came up. High waves were breaking into the boat, and it began to fill with water.

Jesus was sleeping at the back of the boat with his head on a cushion. The disciples woke him up, shouting, "Teacher, don't you care that we're going to drown?"

When Jesus woke up, he rebuked the wind and said to the waves, "Silence! Be still!" Suddenly the wind stopped, and there was a great calm. Then he asked them, "Why are you afraid? Do you still have no faith?"

The disciples were absolutely terrified. "Who is this man?" they asked each other. "Even the wind and waves obey him!"

Mark 4:35–41 (NLT)

# Jesus Brings a Girl Back to Life

## Luke 8

THEN A MAN NAMED JAIRUS, a leader of the local synagogue, came and fell at Jesus' feet, pleading with him to come home with him. His only daughter, who was about twelve years old, was dying.

As Jesus went with him, he was surrounded by the crowds. A woman in the crowd had suffered for twelve years with constant bleeding, and she could find no cure. Coming up behind Jesus, she touched the fringe of his robe. Immediately, the bleeding stopped.

"Who touched me?" Jesus asked.

Everyone denied it, and Peter said, "Master, this whole crowd is pressing up against you."

When the woman realized that she could not stay hidden, she began to tremble and fell to her knees in front of him.

"Daughter," he said to her, "your faith has made you well. Go in peace."

While he was still speaking to her, a messenger arrived from the home of Jairus, the leader of the synagogue. He told him, "Your daughter is dead. There's no use troubling the Teacher now."

But when Jesus heard what had happened, he said to Jairus, "Don't be afraid. Just have faith, and she will be healed."

When they arrived at the house, Jesus wouldn't let anyone go in with him except Peter, John, James, and the little girl's father and mother. The house was filled with people weeping and wailing, but he said, "Stop the weeping! She isn't dead; she's only asleep."

But the crowd laughed at him because they all knew she had died. Then Jesus took her by the hand and said in a loud voice, "My child, get up!" And at that moment her life returned, and she immediately stood up! Then Jesus told them to give her something to eat.

Luke 8:41–45, 47–55 (NLT)

# Jesus Feeds More Than 5,000 People

## John 6

AFTER THIS, JESUS CROSSED OVER to the far side of the Sea of Galilee, also known as the Sea of Tiberias. A huge crowd kept following him wherever he went, because they saw his miraculous signs as he healed the sick. Then Jesus climbed a hill and sat down with his disciples around him. Jesus soon saw a huge crowd of people coming to look for him. Turning to Philip, he asked, "Where can we buy bread to feed all these people?" He was testing Philip, for he already knew what he was going to do.

Philip replied, "Even if we worked for months, we wouldn't have enough money to feed them!"

Then Andrew, Simon Peter's brother, spoke up. "There's a young boy here with five barley loaves and two fish. But what good is that with this huge crowd?"

"Tell everyone to sit down," Jesus said. So they all sat down on the grassy slopes. (The men alone numbered about 5,000.) Then Jesus took the loaves, gave thanks to God, and distributed them to the people. Afterward he did the same with the fish. And they all ate as much as they wanted. After everyone was full, Jesus told his disciples, "Now gather the leftovers, so that nothing is wasted." So they picked up the pieces and filled twelve baskets with scraps left by the people who had eaten from the five barley loaves.

John 6:1–3, 5–13 (NLT)

# Jesus Walks on Water

## Mark 6

AT ONCE JESUS made his disciples get into the boat and go ahead of him to Bethsaida, on the other side of the lake, while he sent the crowd away. After saying good-bye to the people, he went away to a hill to pray. When evening came, the boat was in the middle of the lake, while Jesus was alone on land. He saw that his disciples were straining at the oars, because they were rowing against the wind; so sometime between three and six o'clock in the morning, he came to them, walking on the water. He was going to pass them by, but they saw him walking on the water. "It's a ghost!" they thought, and screamed. They were all terrified when they saw him.

Jesus spoke to them at once, "Courage!" he said. "It is I. Don't be afraid!" Then he got into the boat with them, and the wind died down. The disciples were completely amazed, because they had not understood the real meaning of the feeding of the five thousand; their minds could not grasp it.

Mark 6:45–52 (GNT)

CLEVELAND
WOODWARD

# Jesus Restores a Man's Hearing

## Mark 7

JESUS LEFT TYRE and went up to Sidon before going back to the Sea of Galilee and the region of the Ten Towns. A deaf man with a speech impediment was brought to him, and the people begged Jesus to lay his hands on the man to heal him.

Jesus led him away from the crowd so they could be alone. He put his fingers into the man's ears. Then, spitting on his own fingers, he touched the man's tongue. Looking up to heaven, he sighed and said, *"Ephphatha,"* which means, "Be opened!" Instantly the man could hear perfectly, and his tongue was freed so he could speak plainly!

Jesus told the crowd not to tell anyone, but the more he told them not to, the more they spread the news. They were completely amazed and said again and again, "Everything he does is wonderful. He even makes the deaf to hear and gives speech to those who cannot speak."

Mark 7:31–37 (NLT)

# The Transfiguration

## Matthew 17

SIX DAYS LATER JESUS took Peter and the two brothers, James and John, and led them up a high mountain to be alone. As the men watched, Jesus' appearance was transformed so that his face shone like the sun, and his clothes became as white as light. Suddenly, Moses and Elijah appeared and began talking with Jesus.

Peter exclaimed, "Lord, it's wonderful for us to be here! If you want, I'll make three shelters as memorials—one for you, one for Moses, and one for Elijah."

But even as he spoke, a bright cloud overshadowed them, and a voice from the cloud said, "This is my dearly loved Son, who brings me great joy. Listen to him." The disciples were terrified and fell face down on the ground.

Then Jesus came over and touched them. "Get up," he said. "Don't be afraid." And when they looked up, Moses and Elijah were gone, and they saw only Jesus.

As they went back down the mountain, Jesus commanded them, "Don't tell anyone what you have seen until the Son of Man has been raised from the dead."

Matthew 17:1–9 (NLT)

# Jesus Tells an Evil Spirit to Leave

## Mark 9

AND WHEN [Jesus, Peter, James, and John] came to the disciples, they saw a great crowd around them, and scribes arguing with them.

And [Jesus] asked them, "What are you arguing about with them?" And someone from the crowd answered him, "Teacher, I brought my son to you, for he has a spirit that makes him mute. And whenever it seizes him, it throws him down, and he foams and grinds his teeth and becomes rigid. So I asked your disciples to cast it out, and they were not able."

And they brought the boy to him. And when the spirit saw him, immediately it convulsed the boy, and he fell on the ground and rolled about, foaming at the mouth. And Jesus asked his father, "How long has this been happening to him?" And he said, "From childhood. And it has often cast him into fire and into water, to destroy him. But if you can do anything, have compassion on us and help us." And Jesus said to him, "'If you can'! All things are possible for one who believes." Immediately the father of the child cried out and said, "I believe; help my unbelief!" And when Jesus saw that a crowd came running together, he rebuked the unclean spirit, saying to it, "You mute and deaf spirit, I command you, come out of him and never enter him again." And after crying out and convulsing him terribly, it came out, and the boy was like a corpse, so that most of them said, "He is dead." But Jesus took him by the hand and lifted him up, and he arose.

Mark 9:14, 16–18, 20–27 (ESV)

# Jesus Heals a Man Born Blind

## John 9

AS JESUS WAS WALKING ALONG, he saw a man who had been blind from birth. "Rabbi," his disciples asked him, "why was this man born blind? Was it because of his own sins or his parents' sins?"

"It was not because of his sins or his parents' sins," Jesus answered. "This happened so the power of God could be seen in him. We must quickly carry out the tasks assigned us by the one who sent us. The night is coming, and then no one can work. But while I am here in the world, I am the light of the world."

Then he spit on the ground, made mud with the saliva, and spread the mud over the blind man's eyes. He told him, "Go wash yourself in the pool of Siloam" (Siloam means "sent"). So the man went and washed and came back seeing!

His neighbors and others who knew him as a blind beggar asked each other, "Isn't this the man who used to sit and beg?" Some said he was, and others said, "No, he just looks like him!"

But the beggar kept saying, "Yes, I am the same one!"

They asked, "Who healed you? What happened?"

He told them, "The man they call Jesus made mud and spread it over my eyes and told me, 'Go to the pool of Siloam and wash yourself.' So I went and washed, and now I can see!"

John 9:1–11 (NLT)

# Jesus Heals a Disabled Woman

## Luke 13

NOW [JESUS] WAS TEACHING in one of the synagogues on the Sabbath. And behold, there was a woman who had had a disabling spirit for eighteen years. She was bent over and could not fully straighten herself. When Jesus saw her, he called her over and said to her, "Woman, you are freed from your disability." And he laid his hands on her, and immediately she was made straight, and she glorified God. But the ruler of the synagogue, indignant because Jesus had healed on the Sabbath, said to the people, "There are six days in which work ought to be done. Come on those days and be healed, and not on the Sabbath day." Then the Lord answered him, "You hypocrites! Does not each of you on the Sabbath untie his ox or his donkey from the manger and lead it away to water it? And ought not this woman, a daughter of Abraham whom Satan bound for eighteen years, be loosed from this bond on the Sabbath day?" As he said these things, all his adversaries were put to shame, and all the people rejoiced at all the glorious things that were done by him.

Luke 13:10–17 (ESV)

# Jesus Raises Lazarus from the Dead

## John 11

A MAN NAMED LAZARUS WAS SICK. He lived in Bethany with his sisters, Mary and Martha.

So the two sisters sent a message to Jesus telling him, "Lord, your dear friend is very sick."

When Jesus arrived at Bethany, he was told that Lazarus had already been in his grave for four days.

When Martha got word that Jesus was coming, she went to meet him. Martha said to Jesus, "Lord, if only you had been here, my brother would not have died. But even now I know that God will give you whatever you ask."

Jesus told her, "Your brother will rise again."

"Yes," Martha said, "he will rise when everyone else rises, at the last day."

Jesus told her, "I am the resurrection and the life. Anyone who believes in me will live, even after dying."

When Mary arrived and saw Jesus, she fell at his feet and said, "Lord, if only you had been here, my brother would not have died."

"Where have you put him?" he asked them.

They told him, "Lord, come and see." Then Jesus wept.

"Roll the stone aside," Jesus told them.

So they rolled the stone aside. Then Jesus looked up to heaven and said, "Father, thank you for hearing me. You always hear me, but I said it out loud for the sake of all these people standing here, so that they will believe you sent me." Then Jesus shouted, "Lazarus, come out!" And the dead man came out, his hands and feet bound in graveclothes, his face wrapped in a headcloth. Jesus told them, "Unwrap him and let him go!"

John 11:1, 3, 17, 20–25, 32, 34–35, 39, 41–44 (NLT)

# Jesus Heals a Thankful Leper

## Luke 17

AS JESUS CONTINUED on toward Jerusalem, he reached the border between Galilee and Samaria. As he entered a village there, ten men with leprosy stood at a distance, crying out, "Jesus, Master, have mercy on us!"

He looked at them and said, "Go show yourselves to the priests." And as they went, they were cleansed of their leprosy.

One of them, when he saw that he was healed, came back to Jesus, shouting, "Praise God!" He fell to the ground at Jesus' feet, thanking him for what he had done. This man was a Samaritan.

Jesus asked, "Didn't I heal ten men? Where are the other nine? Has no one returned to give glory to God except this foreigner?" And Jesus said to the man, "Stand up and go. Your faith has healed you."

Luke 17:11–19 (NLT)

# Jesus Anointed by Mary

## John 12

SIX DAYS BEFORE THE PASSOVER celebration began, Jesus arrived in Bethany, the home of Lazarus—the man he had raised from the dead. A dinner was prepared in Jesus' honor. Martha served, and Lazarus was among those who ate with him. Then Mary took a twelve-ounce jar of expensive perfume made from essence of nard, and she anointed Jesus' feet with it, wiping his feet with her hair. The house was filled with the fragrance.

But Judas Iscariot, the disciple who would soon betray him, said, "That perfume was worth a year's wages. It should have been sold and the money given to the poor." Not that he cared for the poor—he was a thief, and since he was in charge of the disciples' money, he often stole some for himself.

Jesus replied, "Leave her alone. She did this in preparation for my burial. You will always have the poor among you, but you will not always have me."

When all the people heard of Jesus' arrival, they flocked to see him and also to see Lazarus, the man Jesus had raised from the dead.

John 12:1–9 (NLT)

# Jesus' Triumphal Entry

## John 12

THE NEXT DAY, the news that Jesus was on the way to Jerusalem swept through the city. A large crowd of Passover visitors took palm branches and went down the road to meet him. They shouted,

"Praise God!
  Blessings on the one who comes in the name of the LORD!
  Hail to the King of Israel!"

Jesus found a young donkey and rode on it, fulfilling the prophecy that said:

"Don't be afraid, people of Jerusalem.
  Look, your King is coming,
    riding on a donkey's colt."

His disciples didn't understand at the time that this was a fulfillment of prophecy. But after Jesus entered into his glory, they remembered what had happened and realized that these things had been written about him.

Many in the crowd had seen Jesus call Lazarus from the tomb, raising him from the dead, and they were telling others about it. That was the reason so many went out to meet him—because they had heard about this miraculous sign. Then the Pharisees said to each other, "There's nothing we can do. Look, everyone has gone after him!"

John 12:12–19 (NLT)

CLEVELAND
WOODWARD

# Jesus Clears Out the Temple

## Mark 11

WHEN THEY ARRIVED BACK IN JERUSALEM, Jesus entered the Temple and began to drive out the people buying and selling animals for sacrifices. He knocked over the tables of the money changers and the chairs of those selling doves, and he stopped everyone from using the Temple as a marketplace. He said to them, "The Scriptures declare, 'My Temple will be called a house of prayer for all nations,' but you have turned it into a den of thieves."

When the leading priests and teachers of religious law heard what Jesus had done, they began planning how to kill him. But they were afraid of him because the people were so amazed at his teaching.

That evening Jesus and the disciples left the city.

Mark 11:15–19 (NLT)

# Jesus Washes His Disciples' Feet

## John 13

BEFORE THE PASSOVER CELEBRATION, Jesus knew that his hour had come to leave this world and return to his Father. He had loved his disciples during his ministry on earth, and now he loved them to the very end. It was time for supper, and the devil had already prompted Judas, son of Simon Iscariot, to betray Jesus. Jesus knew that the Father had given him authority over everything and that he had come from God and would return to God. So he got up from the table, took off his robe, wrapped a towel around his waist, and poured water into a basin. Then he began to wash the disciples' feet, drying them with the towel he had around him.

When Jesus came to Simon Peter, Peter said to him, "Lord, are you going to wash my feet?"

Jesus replied, "You don't understand now what I am doing, but someday you will."

"No," Peter protested, "you will never ever wash my feet!"

Jesus replied, "Unless I wash you, you won't belong to me."

Simon Peter exclaimed, "Then wash my hands and head as well, Lord, not just my feet!"

Jesus replied, "A person who has bathed all over does not need to wash, except for the feet, to be entirely clean. And you disciples are clean, but not all of you." For Jesus knew who would betray him. That is what he meant when he said, "Not all of you are clean."

"And since I, your Lord and Teacher, have washed your feet, you ought to wash each other's feet. I have given you an example to follow. Do as I have done to you."

John 13:1–11, 14–15 (NLT)

# The Last Supper

## Mark 14

IN THE EVENING JESUS arrived with the Twelve. As they were at the table eating, Jesus said, "I tell you the truth, one of you eating with me here will betray me."

Greatly distressed, each one asked in turn, "Am I the one?"

He replied, "It is one of you twelve who is eating from this bowl with me. For the Son of Man must die, as the Scriptures declared long ago. But how terrible it will be for the one who betrays him. It would be far better for that man if he had never been born!"

As they were eating, Jesus took some bread and blessed it. Then he broke it in pieces and gave it to the disciples, saying, "Take it, for this is my body."

And he took a cup of wine and gave thanks to God for it. He gave it to them, and they all drank from it. And he said to them, "This is my blood, which confirms the covenant between God and his people. It is poured out as a sacrifice for many. I tell you the truth, I will not drink wine again until the day I drink it new in the Kingdom of God."

Then they sang a hymn and went out to the Mount of Olives.

Mark 14:17–26 (NLT)

garo

# Jesus in the Garden of Gethsemane

## Matthew 26

THEN JESUS WENT WITH THEM to the olive grove called Gethsemane, and he said, "Sit here while I go over there to pray." He took Peter and Zebedee's two sons, James and John, and he became anguished and distressed. He told them, "My soul is crushed with grief to the point of death. Stay here and keep watch with me."

He went on a little farther and bowed with his face to the ground, praying, "My Father! If it is possible, let this cup of suffering be taken away from me. Yet I want your will to be done, not mine."

Then he returned to the disciples and found them asleep. He said to Peter, "Couldn't you watch with me even one hour? Keep watch and pray, so that you will not give in to temptation. For the spirit is willing, but the body is weak!"

Then Jesus left them a second time and prayed, "My Father! If this cup cannot be taken away unless I drink it, your will be done." When he returned to them again, he found them sleeping, for they couldn't keep their eyes open.

So he went to pray a third time, saying the same things again. Then he came to the disciples and said, "Go ahead and sleep. Have your rest. But look—the time has come. The Son of Man is betrayed into the hands of sinners. Up, let's be going. Look, my betrayer is here!"

Matthew 26:36–46 (NLT)

# Jesus Is Betrayed and Arrested

## Matthew 26

JUDAS, ONE OF THE TWELVE FOLLOWERS, came while Jesus was talking. He came with many others who had swords and sticks. They came from the religious leaders of the Jews and the leaders of the people. The man who handed Jesus over gave the men something to look for. He said, "The One I kiss is the One you want. Take Him!" At once Judas went up to Jesus and said, "Hello, Teacher," and kissed Him. Jesus said to him, "Friend, do what you came to do." Then they came and put their hands on Jesus and took Him.

One of those with Jesus took his sword. He hit the servant who was owned by the religious leader and cut off his ear. Jesus said to him, "Put your sword back where it belongs. Everyone who uses a sword will die with a sword. Do you not think that I can pray to My Father? At once He would send Me more than 70,000 angels. If I did, how could it happen as the Holy Writings said it would happen? It must be this way."

Then Jesus said to the many people, "Have you come with swords and sticks to take Me as if I were a robber? I have been with you every day teaching in the house of God. You never put your hands on Me then. But this has happened as the early preachers said in the Holy Writings it would happen." Then all the followers left Him and ran away.

Matthew 26:47–56 (NLV)

# The High Priest Questions Jesus

## Matthew 26

THEN THE PEOPLE WHO HAD ARRESTED JESUS led him to the home of Caiaphas, the high priest, where the teachers of religious law and the elders had gathered. Meanwhile, Peter followed him at a distance and came to the high priest's courtyard. He went in and sat with the guards and waited to see how it would all end.

Inside, the leading priests and the entire high council were trying to find witnesses who would lie about Jesus, so they could put him to death. But even though they found many who agreed to give false witness, they could not use anyone's testimony. Finally, two men came forward who declared, "This man said, 'I am able to destroy the Temple of God and rebuild it in three days.'"

Then the high priest stood up and said to Jesus, "Well, aren't you going to answer these charges? What do you have to say for yourself?" But Jesus remained silent. Then the high priest said to him, "I demand in the name of the living God—tell us if you are the Messiah, the Son of God."

Jesus replied, "You have said it. And in the future you will see the Son of Man seated in the place of power at God's right hand and coming on the clouds of heaven."

Then the high priest tore his clothing to show his horror and said, "Blasphemy! Why do we need other witnesses? You have all heard his blasphemy. What is your verdict?"

"Guilty!" they shouted. "He deserves to die!"

Matthew 26:57–66 (NLT)

# Peter Denies Jesus

## Mark 14

MEANWHILE, PETER was in the courtyard below. One of the servant girls who worked for the high priest came by and noticed Peter warming himself at the fire. She looked at him closely and said, "You were one of those with Jesus of Nazareth."

But Peter denied it. "I don't know what you're talking about," he said, and he went out into the entryway. Just then, a rooster crowed.

When the servant girl saw him standing there, she began telling the others, "This man is definitely one of them!" But Peter denied it again.

A little later some of the other bystanders confronted Peter and said, "You must be one of them, because you are a Galilean."

Peter swore, "A curse on me if I'm lying—I don't know this man you're talking about!" And immediately the rooster crowed the second time.

Suddenly, Jesus' words flashed through Peter's mind: "Before the rooster crows twice, you will deny three times that you even know me." And he broke down and wept.

Mark 14:66–72 (NLT)

# Jesus' Trial Before Pilate

## Matthew 27

NOW JESUS WAS STANDING before Pilate, the Roman governor. "Are you the king of the Jews?" the governor asked him.

Jesus replied, "You have said it."

But when the leading priests and the elders made their accusations against him, Jesus remained silent. "Don't you hear all these charges they are bringing against you?" Pilate demanded. But Jesus made no response to any of the charges, much to the governor's surprise.

Now it was the governor's custom each year during the Passover celebration to release one prisoner to the crowd—anyone they wanted. This year there was a notorious prisoner, a man named Barabbas. As the crowds gathered before Pilate's house that morning, he asked them, "Which one do you want me to release to you—Barabbas, or Jesus who is called the Messiah?" (He knew very well that the religious leaders had arrested Jesus out of envy.)

Meanwhile, the leading priests and the elders persuaded the crowd to ask for Barabbas to be released and for Jesus to be put to death. So the governor asked again, "Which of these two do you want me to release to you?"

The crowd shouted back, "Barabbas!"

Pilate responded, "Then what should I do with Jesus who is called the Messiah?"

They shouted back, "Crucify him!"

"Why?" Pilate demanded. "What crime has he committed?"

But the mob roared even louder, "Crucify him!"

Pilate saw that he wasn't getting anywhere and that a riot was developing. So he sent for a bowl of water and washed his hands before the crowd, saying, "I am innocent of this man's blood. The responsibility is yours!"

And all the people yelled back, "We will take responsibility for his death—we and our children!"

Matthew 27:11–18, 20–25 (NLT)

# The Soldiers Mock Jesus

## Matthew 27

SOME OF THE GOVERNOR'S SOLDIERS took Jesus into their headquarters and called out the entire regiment. They stripped him and put a scarlet robe on him. They wove thorn branches into a crown and put it on his head, and they placed a reed stick in his right hand as a scepter. Then they knelt before him in mockery and taunted, "Hail! King of the Jews!" And they spit on him and grabbed the stick and struck him on the head with it. When they were finally tired of mocking him, they took off the robe and put his own clothes on him again.

Matthew 27:27–31 (NLT)

CLEVELAND
WOODWARD

# Jesus Rejected by the Crowd

## John 19

PILATE WENT OUT AGAIN and said to them, "See, I am bringing him out to you that you may know that I find no guilt in him." So Jesus came out, wearing the crown of thorns and the purple robe. Pilate said to them, "Behold the man!" When the chief priests and the officers saw him, they cried out, "Crucify him, crucify him!" Pilate said to them, "Take him yourselves and crucify him, for I find no guilt in him." The Jews answered him, "We have a law, and according to that law he ought to die because he has made himself the Son of God." When Pilate heard this statement, he was even more afraid. He entered his headquarters again and said to Jesus, "Where are you from?" But Jesus gave him no answer. So Pilate said to him, "You will not speak to me? Do you not know that I have authority to release you and authority to crucify you?" Jesus answered him, "You would have no authority over me at all unless it had been given you from above. Therefore he who delivered me over to you has the greater sin."

From then on Pilate sought to release him, but the Jews cried out, "If you release this man, you are not Caesar's friend. Everyone who makes himself a king opposes Caesar." So when Pilate heard these words, he brought Jesus out and sat down on the judgment seat at a place called The Stone Pavement, and in Aramaic Gabbatha. Now it was the day of Preparation of the Passover. It was about the sixth hour. He said to the Jews, "Behold your King!" They cried out, "Away with him, away with him, crucify him!" Pilate said to them, "Shall I crucify your King?" The chief priests answered, "We have no king but Caesar." So he delivered him over to them to be crucified.

John 19:4–16 (ESV)

# Simon of Cyrene Helps Jesus

## Luke 23

AS THEY LED JESUS AWAY, a man named Simon, who was from Cyrene, happened to be coming in from the countryside. The soldiers seized him and put the cross on him and made him carry it behind Jesus. A large crowd trailed behind, including many grief-stricken women.

Luke 23:26–27 (NLT)

# Jesus Nailed to a Cross

## Luke 23

WHEN THE SOLDIERS CAME TO THE PLACE called "The Skull," they nailed Jesus to a cross. They also nailed the two criminals to crosses, one on each side of Jesus.

Jesus said, "Father, forgive these people! They don't know what they're doing."

While the crowd stood there watching Jesus, the soldiers gambled for his clothes. The leaders insulted him by saying, "He saved others. Now he should save himself, if he really is God's chosen Messiah!"

The soldiers made fun of Jesus and brought him some wine. They said, "If you are the king of the Jews, save yourself!"

Above him was a sign that said, "This is the King of the Jews."

One of the criminals hanging there also insulted Jesus by saying, "Aren't you the Messiah? Save yourself and save us!"

But the other criminal told the first one off, "Don't you fear God? Aren't you getting the same punishment as this man? We got what was coming to us, but he didn't do anything wrong." Then he said to Jesus, "Remember me when you come into power!"

Jesus replied, "I promise that today you will be with me in paradise."

Luke 23:33–43 (CEV)

# When Jesus Died

## Mark 15

AT NOON, DARKNESS FELL across the whole land until three o'clock. Then at three o'clock Jesus called out with a loud voice, *"Eloi, Eloi, lema sabachthani?"* which means "My God, my God, why have you abandoned me?"

Some of the bystanders misunderstood and thought he was calling for the prophet Elijah. One of them ran and filled a sponge with sour wine, holding it up to him on a reed stick so he could drink. "Wait!" he said. "Let's see whether Elijah comes to take him down!"

Then Jesus uttered another loud cry and breathed his last. And the curtain in the sanctuary of the Temple was torn in two, from top to bottom.

When the Roman officer who stood facing him saw how he had died, he exclaimed, "This man truly was the Son of God!"

Some women were there, watching from a distance, including Mary Magdalene, Mary (the mother of James the younger and of Joseph), and Salome. They had been followers of Jesus and had cared for him while he was in Galilee. Many other women who had come with him to Jerusalem were also there.

Mark 15:33–41 (NLT)

# Jesus Placed in the Tomb

## Luke 23

NOW THERE WAS A GOOD and righteous man named Joseph. He was a member of the Jewish high council, but he had not agreed with the decision and actions of the other religious leaders. He was from the town of Arimathea in Judea, and he was waiting for the Kingdom of God to come. He went to Pilate and asked for Jesus' body. Then he took the body down from the cross and wrapped it in a long sheet of linen cloth and laid it in a new tomb that had been carved out of rock. This was done late on Friday afternoon, the day of preparation, as the Sabbath was about to begin.

As his body was taken away, the women from Galilee followed and saw the tomb where his body was placed. Then they went home and prepared spices and ointments to anoint his body. But by the time they were finished the Sabbath had begun, so they rested as required by the law.

Luke 23:50–56 (NLT)

# The Resurrection

## Mark 16

SATURDAY EVENING, when the Sabbath ended, Mary Magdalene, Mary the mother of James, and Salome went out and purchased burial spices so they could anoint Jesus' body. Very early on Sunday morning, just at sunrise, they went to the tomb. On the way they were asking each other, "Who will roll away the stone for us from the entrance to the tomb?" But as they arrived, they looked up and saw that the stone, which was very large, had already been rolled aside.

When they entered the tomb, they saw a young man clothed in a white robe sitting on the right side. The women were shocked, but the angel said, "Don't be alarmed. You are looking for Jesus of Nazareth, who was crucified. He isn't here! He is risen from the dead! Look, this is where they laid his body. Now go and tell his disciples, including Peter, that Jesus is going ahead of you to Galilee. You will see him there, just as he told you before he died."

Mark 16:1–7 (NLT)

# Peter and John at the Tomb

## John 20

EARLY ON SUNDAY MORNING, while it was still dark, Mary Magdalene came to the tomb and found that the stone had been rolled away from the entrance. She ran and found Simon Peter and the other disciple, the one whom Jesus loved. She said, "They have taken the Lord's body out of the tomb, and we don't know where they have put him!"

Peter and the other disciple started out for the tomb. They were both running, but the other disciple outran Peter and reached the tomb first. He stooped and looked in and saw the linen wrappings lying there, but he didn't go in. Then Simon Peter arrived and went inside. He also noticed the linen wrappings lying there, while the cloth that had covered Jesus' head was folded up and lying apart from the other wrappings. Then the disciple who had reached the tomb first also went in, and he saw and believed—for until then they still hadn't understood the Scriptures that said Jesus must rise from the dead.

John 20:1–9 (NLT)

# Jesus Appears to Mary Magdalene

## John 20

MARY WAS STANDING OUTSIDE the tomb crying, and as she wept, she stooped and looked in. She saw two white-robed angels, one sitting at the head and the other at the foot of the place where the body of Jesus had been lying. "Dear woman, why are you crying?" the angels asked her.

"Because they have taken away my Lord," she replied, "and I don't know where they have put him."

She turned to leave and saw someone standing there. It was Jesus, but she didn't recognize him. "Dear woman, why are you crying?" Jesus asked her. "Who are you looking for?"

She thought he was the gardener. "Sir," she said, "if you have taken him away, tell me where you have put him, and I will go and get him."

"Mary!" Jesus said.

She turned to him and cried out, "Rabboni!" (which is Hebrew for "Teacher").

"Don't cling to me," Jesus said, "for I haven't yet ascended to the Father. But go find my brothers and tell them, 'I am ascending to my Father and your Father, to my God and your God.'"

Mary Magdalene found the disciples and told them, "I have seen the Lord!" Then she gave them his message.

John 20:11–18 (NLT)

# Two Disciples Meet Jesus on the Road

## Luke 24

THAT VERY DAY two of [Jesus' followers] were going to a village named Emmaus, about seven miles from Jerusalem, and they were talking with each other about all these things that had happened. While they were talking and discussing together, Jesus himself drew near and went with them. But their eyes were kept from recognizing him. And he said to them, "What is this conversation that you are holding with each other as you walk?" And they stood still, looking sad. Then one of them, named Cleopas, answered him, "Are you the only visitor to Jerusalem who does not know the things that have happened there in these days?" And he said to them, "What things?" And they said to him, "Concerning Jesus of Nazareth, a man who was a prophet mighty in deed and word before God and all the people, and how our chief priests and rulers delivered him up to be condemned to death, and crucified him. But we had hoped that he was the one to redeem Israel. Yes, and besides all this, it is now the third day since these things happened. Moreover, some women of our company amazed us. They were at the tomb early in the morning, and when they did not find his body, they came back saying that they had even seen a vision of angels, who said that he was alive. Some of those who were with us went to the tomb and found it just as the women had said, but him they did not see." And he said to them, "O foolish ones, and slow of heart to believe all that the prophets have spoken! Was it not necessary that the Christ should suffer these things and enter into his glory?" And beginning with Moses and all the Prophets, he interpreted to them in all the Scriptures the things concerning himself.

Luke 24:13–27 (ESV)

# Jesus Revealed to Two Disciples

## Luke 24

BY THIS TIME [Jesus and the two disciples] were nearing Emmaus and the end of their journey. Jesus acted as if he were going on, but they begged him, "Stay the night with us, since it is getting late." So he went home with them. As they sat down to eat, he took the bread and blessed it. Then he broke it and gave it to them. Suddenly, their eyes were opened, and they recognized him. And at that moment he disappeared!

They said to each other, "Didn't our hearts burn within us as he talked with us on the road and explained the Scriptures to us?" And within the hour they were on their way back to Jerusalem. There they found the eleven disciples and the others who had gathered with them, who said, "The Lord has really risen! He appeared to Peter."

Luke 24:28–34 (NLT)

# Jesus Appears to the Disciples

## Luke 24

THEN THE TWO FROM EMMAUS told their story of how Jesus had appeared to them as they were walking along the road, and how they had recognized him as he was breaking the bread. And just as they were telling about it, Jesus himself was suddenly standing there among them. "Peace be with you," he said. But the whole group was startled and frightened, thinking they were seeing a ghost!

"Why are you frightened?" he asked. "Why are your hearts filled with doubt? Look at my hands. Look at my feet. You can see that it's really me. Touch me and make sure that I am not a ghost, because ghosts don't have bodies, as you see that I do." As he spoke, he showed them his hands and his feet.

Still they stood there in disbelief, filled with joy and wonder. Then he asked them, "Do you have anything here to eat?" They gave him a piece of broiled fish, and he ate it as they watched.

Then he said, "When I was with you before, I told you that everything written about me in the law of Moses and the prophets and in the Psalms must be fulfilled." Then he opened their minds to understand the Scriptures. And he said, "Yes, it was written long ago that the Messiah would suffer and die and rise from the dead on the third day. It was also written that this message would be proclaimed in the authority of his name to all the nations, beginning in Jerusalem: 'There is forgiveness of sins for all who repent.' You are witnesses of all these things.

"And now I will send the Holy Spirit, just as my Father promised. But stay here in the city until the Holy Spirit comes and fills you with power from heaven."

Luke 24:35–49 (NLT)

# Jesus Appears to Thomas

## John 20

One of the twelve disciples, Thomas (nicknamed the Twin), was not with the others when Jesus came. They told him, "We have seen the Lord!"

But he replied, "I won't believe it unless I see the nail wounds in his hands, put my fingers into them, and place my hand into the wound in his side."

Eight days later the disciples were together again, and this time Thomas was with them. The doors were locked; but suddenly, as before, Jesus was standing among them. "Peace be with you," he said. Then he said to Thomas, "Put your finger here, and look at my hands. Put your hand into the wound in my side. Don't be faithless any longer. Believe!"

"My Lord and my God!" Thomas exclaimed.

Then Jesus told him, "You believe because you have seen me. Blessed are those who believe without seeing me."

The disciples saw Jesus do many other miraculous signs in addition to the ones recorded in this book. But these are written so that you may continue to believe that Jesus is the Messiah, the Son of God, and that by believing in him you will have life by the power of his name.

John 20:24–31 (NLT)

# A Miraculous Catch

## John 21

LATER, JESUS APPEARED AGAIN to the disciples beside the Sea of Galilee. This is how it happened. Several of the disciples were there—Simon Peter, Thomas (nicknamed the Twin), Nathanael from Cana in Galilee, the sons of Zebedee, and two other disciples.

Simon Peter said, "I'm going fishing."

"We'll come, too," they all said. So they went out in the boat, but they caught nothing all night.

At dawn Jesus was standing on the beach, but the disciples couldn't see who he was. He called out, "Fellows, have you caught any fish?"

"No," they replied.

Then he said, "Throw out your net on the right-hand side of the boat, and you'll get some!" So they did, and they couldn't haul in the net because there were so many fish in it.

Then the disciple Jesus loved said to Peter, "It's the Lord!" When Simon Peter heard that it was the Lord, he put on his tunic (for he had stripped for work), jumped into the water, and headed to shore. The others stayed with the boat and pulled the loaded net to the shore, for they were only about a hundred yards from shore. When they got there, they found breakfast waiting for them—fish cooking over a charcoal fire, and some bread.

"Bring some of the fish you've just caught," Jesus said. So Simon Peter went aboard and dragged the net to the shore. There were 153 large fish, and yet the net hadn't torn.

"Now come and have some breakfast!" Jesus said. None of the disciples dared to ask him, "Who are you?" They knew it was the Lord. Then Jesus served them the bread and the fish. This was the third time Jesus had appeared to his disciples since he had been raised from the dead.

John 21:1–14 (NLT)

# Peter Is Restored

## John 21

AFTER BREAKFAST JESUS ASKED SIMON PETER, "Simon son of John, do you love me more than these?"

"Yes, Lord," Peter replied, "you know I love you."

"Then feed my lambs," Jesus told him.

Jesus repeated the question: "Simon son of John, do you love me?"

"Yes, Lord," Peter said, "you know I love you."

"Then take care of my sheep," Jesus said.

A third time he asked him, "Simon son of John, do you love me?"

Peter was hurt that Jesus asked the question a third time. He said, "Lord, you know everything. You know that I love you."

Jesus said, "Then feed my sheep.

"I tell you the truth, when you were young, you were able to do as you liked; you dressed yourself and went wherever you wanted to go. But when you are old, you will stretch out your hands, and others will dress you and take you where you don't want to go." Jesus said this to let him know by what kind of death he would glorify God. Then Jesus told him, "Follow me."

Peter turned around and saw behind them the disciple Jesus loved—the one who had leaned over to Jesus during supper and asked, "Lord, who will betray you?" Peter asked Jesus, "What about him, Lord?"

Jesus replied, "If I want him to remain alive until I return, what is that to you? As for you, follow me."

Jesus also did many other things. If they were all written down, I suppose the whole world could not contain the books that would be written.

John 21:15–22, 25 (NLT)

# The Great Commission

## Matthew 28

THEN THE ELEVEN DISCIPLES left for Galilee, going to the mountain where Jesus had told them to go. When they saw him, they worshiped him—but some of them doubted!

Jesus came and told his disciples, "I have been given all authority in heaven and on earth. Therefore, go and make disciples of all the nations, baptizing them in the name of the Father and the Son and the Holy Spirit. Teach these new disciples to obey all the commands I have given you. And be sure of this: I am with you always, even to the end of the age."

Matthew 28:16–20 (NLT)

# Jesus Ascends into Heaven

## Acts 1

SO WHEN THE APOSTLES were with Jesus, they kept asking him, "Lord, has the time come for you to free Israel and restore our kingdom?"

He replied, "The Father alone has the authority to set those dates and times, and they are not for you to know. But you will receive power when the Holy Spirit comes upon you. And you will be my witnesses, telling people about me everywhere—in Jerusalem, throughout Judea, in Samaria, and to the ends of the earth."

After saying this, he was taken up into a cloud while they were watching, and they could no longer see him. As they strained to see him rising into heaven, two white-robed men suddenly stood among them. "Men of Galilee," they said, "why are you standing here staring into heaven? Jesus has been taken from you into heaven, but someday he will return from heaven in the same way you saw him go!"

Acts 1:6–11 (NLT)

CLEVELAND
WOODWARD

# The Holy Spirit Comes

## Acts 2

ON THE DAY OF PENTECOST all the believers were meeting together in one place. Suddenly, there was a sound from heaven like the roaring of a mighty windstorm, and it filled the house where they were sitting. Then, what looked like flames or tongues of fire appeared and settled on each of them. And everyone present was filled with the Holy Spirit and began speaking in other languages, as the Holy Spirit gave them this ability.

At that time there were devout Jews from every nation living in Jerusalem. When they heard the loud noise, everyone came running, and they were bewildered to hear their own languages being spoken by the believers.

They were completely amazed. "How can this be?" they exclaimed. "These people are all from Galilee, and yet we hear them speaking in our own native languages! Here we are—Parthians, Medes, Elamites, people from Mesopotamia, Judea, Cappadocia, Pontus, the province of Asia, Phrygia, Pamphylia, Egypt, and the areas of Libya around Cyrene, visitors from Rome (both Jews and converts to Judaism), Cretans, and Arabs. And we all hear these people speaking in our own languages about the wonderful things God has done!" They stood there amazed and perplexed. "What can this mean?" they asked each other.

Acts 2:1–12 (NLT)

# Peter Preaches with Power

## Acts 2

THEN PETER STEPPED FORWARD with the eleven other apostles and shouted to the crowd, "Listen carefully, all of you, fellow Jews and residents of Jerusalem! Make no mistake about this. These people are not drunk, as some of you are assuming. No, what you see was predicted long ago by the prophet Joel:

'In the last days,' God says,
'I will pour out my Spirit upon all people.
In those days I will pour out my Spirit
even on my servants—men and women alike—
and they will prophesy.
The sun will become dark,
and the moon will turn blood red
before that great and glorious day of the LORD arrives.
But everyone who calls on the name of the LORD
will be saved.'

"People of Israel, listen! God publicly endorsed Jesus the Nazarene by doing powerful miracles, wonders, and signs through him, as you well know.

"God raised Jesus from the dead, and we are all witnesses of this.

"So let everyone in Israel know for certain that God has made this Jesus, whom you crucified, to be both Lord and Messiah!"

Peter's words pierced their hearts, and they said to him and to the other apostles, "Brothers, what should we do?"

Peter replied, "Each of you must repent of your sins and turn to God, and be baptized in the name of Jesus Christ for the forgiveness of your sins. Then you will receive the gift of the Holy Spirit."

Those who believed what Peter said were baptized and added to the church that day—about 3,000 in all.

Acts 2:14–18, 20–22, 32, 36–38, 41 (NLT)

C.L. WOOD

# Believers Help One Another

## Acts 2 and 4

ALL THE BELIEVERS DEVOTED THEMSELVES to the apostles' teaching, and to fellowship, and to sharing in meals (including the Lord's Supper), and to prayer.

A deep sense of awe came over them all, and the apostles performed many miraculous signs and wonders. And all the believers met together in one place and shared everything they had. They sold their property and possessions and shared the money with those in need. They worshiped together at the Temple each day, met in homes for the Lord's Supper, and shared their meals with great joy and generosity—all the while praising God and enjoying the goodwill of all the people. And each day the Lord added to their fellowship those who were being saved.

### THE BELIEVERS SHARE THEIR POSSESSIONS

All the believers were united in heart and mind. And they felt that what they owned was not their own, so they shared everything they had. The apostles testified powerfully to the resurrection of the Lord Jesus, and God's great blessing was upon them all. There were no needy people among them, because those who owned land or houses would sell them and bring the money to the apostles to give to those in need.

For instance, there was Joseph, the one the apostles nicknamed Barnabas (which means "Son of Encouragement"). He was from the tribe of Levi and came from the island of Cyprus. He sold a field he owned and brought the money to the apostles.

Acts 2:42–47; 4:32–37 (NLT)

# Peter Heals a Beggar Born Lame

## Acts 3

PETER AND JOHN went to the Temple one afternoon to take part in the three o'clock prayer service. As they approached the Temple, a man lame from birth was being carried in. Each day he was put beside the Temple gate, the one called the Beautiful Gate, so he could beg from the people going into the Temple. When he saw Peter and John about to enter, he asked them for some money.

Peter and John looked at him intently, and Peter said, "Look at us!" The lame man looked at them eagerly, expecting some money. But Peter said, "I don't have any silver or gold for you. But I'll give you what I have. In the name of Jesus Christ the Nazarene, get up and walk!"

Then Peter took the lame man by the right hand and helped him up. And as he did, the man's feet and ankles were instantly healed and strengthened. He jumped up, stood on his feet, and began to walk! Then, walking, leaping, and praising God, he went into the Temple with them.

All the people saw him walking and heard him praising God. When they realized he was the lame beggar they had seen so often at the Beautiful Gate, they were absolutely astounded! They all rushed out in amazement to Solomon's Colonnade, where the man was holding tightly to Peter and John.

Acts 3:1–11 (NLT)

# Philip and the Ethiopian Official

## Acts 8

THE LORD'S ANGEL SAID TO PHILIP, "Go south along the desert road that leads from Jerusalem to Gaza." So Philip left.

An important Ethiopian official happened to be going along that road in his chariot. The official had gone to Jerusalem to worship and was now on his way home. He was sitting in his chariot, reading the book of the prophet Isaiah.

The Spirit told Philip to catch up with the chariot. Philip ran up close and heard the man reading aloud from the book of Isaiah. Philip asked him, "Do you understand what you are reading?"

The official answered, "How can I understand unless someone helps me?" He then invited Philip to come up and sit beside him.

The man was reading the passage that said,

"He was led like a sheep
    on its way to be killed.
He was silent as a lamb
whose wool
    is being cut off,
and he did not say
    a word.
He was treated like a nobody
and did not receive
    a fair trial."

The official said to Philip, "Tell me, was the prophet talking about himself or about someone else?" So Philip began at this place in the Scriptures and explained the good news about Jesus.

As they were going along the road, they came to a place where there was some water. The official said, "Look! Here is some water. Why can't I be baptized?" He ordered the chariot to stop. Then they both went down into the water, and Philip baptized him.

Acts 8:26–38 (CEV)

# Jesus Speaks to Saul

## Acts 9

MEANWHILE, SAUL was uttering threats with every breath and was eager to kill the Lord's followers. So he went to the high priest. He requested letters addressed to the synagogues in Damascus, asking for their cooperation in the arrest of any followers of the Way he found there. He wanted to bring them—both men and women—back to Jerusalem in chains.

As he was approaching Damascus on this mission, a light from heaven suddenly shone down around him. He fell to the ground and heard a voice saying to him, "Saul! Saul! Why are you persecuting me?"

"Who are you, lord?" Saul asked.

And the voice replied, "I am Jesus, the one you are persecuting! Now get up and go into the city, and you will be told what you must do."

The men with Saul stood speechless, for they heard the sound of someone's voice but saw no one! Saul picked himself up off the ground, but when he opened his eyes he was blind. So his companions led him by the hand to Damascus. He remained there blind for three days and did not eat or drink.

Acts 9:1–9 (NLT)

# Ananias Restores Saul's Sight

## Acts 9

NOW THERE WAS A BELIEVER in Damascus named Ananias. The Lord spoke to him in a vision, calling, "Ananias!"

"Yes, Lord!" he replied.

The Lord said, "Go over to Straight Street, to the house of Judas. When you get there, ask for a man from Tarsus named Saul. He is praying to me right now. I have shown him a vision of a man named Ananias coming in and laying hands on him so he can see again."

"But Lord," exclaimed Ananias, "I've heard many people talk about the terrible things this man has done to the believers in Jerusalem! And he is authorized by the leading priests to arrest everyone who calls upon your name."

But the Lord said, "Go, for Saul is my chosen instrument to take my message to the Gentiles and to kings, as well as to the people of Israel. And I will show him how much he must suffer for my name's sake."

So Ananias went and found Saul. He laid his hands on him and said, "Brother Saul, the Lord Jesus, who appeared to you on the road, has sent me so that you might regain your sight and be filled with the Holy Spirit." Instantly something like scales fell from Saul's eyes, and he regained his sight. Then he got up and was baptized. Afterward he ate some food and regained his strength.

Acts 9:10–19 (NLT)

# Saul's Escape from Damascus

## Acts 9

SAUL STAYED WITH THE BELIEVERS in Damascus for a few days. And immediately he began preaching about Jesus in the synagogues, saying, "He is indeed the Son of God!"

All who heard him were amazed. "Isn't this the same man who caused such devastation among Jesus' followers in Jerusalem?" they asked. "And didn't he come here to arrest them and take them in chains to the leading priests?"

Saul's preaching became more and more powerful, and the Jews in Damascus couldn't refute his proofs that Jesus was indeed the Messiah. After a while some of the Jews plotted together to kill him. They were watching for him day and night at the city gate so they could murder him, but Saul was told about their plot. So during the night, some of the other believers lowered him in a large basket through an opening in the city wall.

Acts 9:19–25 (NLT)

# Barnabas Befriends Saul

## Acts 9 and 11

WHEN SAUL ARRIVED IN JERUSALEM, he tried to meet with the believers, but they were all afraid of him. They did not believe he had truly become a believer! Then Barnabas brought him to the apostles and told them how Saul had seen the Lord on the way to Damascus and how the Lord had spoken to Saul. He also told them that Saul had preached boldly in the name of Jesus in Damascus.

So Saul stayed with the apostles and went all around Jerusalem with them, preaching boldly in the name of the Lord.

### THE CHURCH IN ANTIOCH OF SYRIA

Meanwhile, the believers who had been scattered during the persecution after Stephen's death traveled as far as Phoenicia, Cyprus, and Antioch of Syria. They preached the word of God, but only to Jews. However, some of the believers who went to Antioch from Cyprus and Cyrene began preaching to the Gentiles about the Lord Jesus. The power of the Lord was with them, and a large number of these Gentiles believed and turned to the Lord.

When the church at Jerusalem heard what had happened, they sent Barnabas to Antioch. When he arrived and saw this evidence of God's blessing, he was filled with joy, and he encouraged the believers to stay true to the Lord. Barnabas was a good man, full of the Holy Spirit and strong in faith. And many people were brought to the Lord.

Then Barnabas went on to Tarsus to look for Saul. When he found him, he brought him back to Antioch. Both of them stayed there with the church for a full year, teaching large crowds of people. (It was at Antioch that the believers were first called Christians.)

Acts 9:26–28; 11:19–26 (NLT)

C.L. WOODWARD

# Tabitha Raised to Life

## Acts 9

THERE WAS A BELIEVER IN JOPPA NAMED TABITHA (which in Greek is Dorcas). She was always doing kind things for others and helping the poor. About this time she became ill and died. Her body was washed for burial and laid in an upstairs room. But the believers had heard that Peter was nearby at Lydda, so they sent two men to beg him, "Please come as soon as possible!"

So Peter returned with them; and as soon as he arrived, they took him to the upstairs room. The room was filled with widows who were weeping and showing him the coats and other clothes Dorcas had made for them. But Peter asked them all to leave the room; then he knelt and prayed. Turning to the body he said, "Get up, Tabitha." And she opened her eyes! When she saw Peter, she sat up! He gave her his hand and helped her up. Then he called in the widows and all the believers, and he presented her to them alive.

The news spread through the whole town, and many believed in the Lord. And Peter stayed a long time in Joppa, living with Simon, a tanner of hides.

Acts 9:36–43 (NLT)

# Peter's Daydream

## Acts 10

THERE WAS A MAN IN CAESAREA NAMED CORNELIUS, who was a captain in the Roman army regiment called "The Italian Regiment." He was a religious man; he and his whole family worshiped God. He also did much to help the Jewish poor people and was constantly praying to God. It was about three o'clock one afternoon when he had a vision, in which he clearly saw an angel of God come in and say to him, "Cornelius!"

He stared at the angel in fear and said, "What is it, sir?"

The angel answered, "God is pleased with your prayers and works of charity, and is ready to answer you. And now send some men to Joppa for a certain man whose full name is Simon Peter."

The next day, as they were on their way and coming near Joppa, Peter went up on the roof of the house about noon in order to pray. He became hungry and wanted something to eat; while the food was being prepared, he had a vision. He saw heaven opened and something coming down that looked like a large sheet being lowered by its four corners to the earth. In it were all kinds of animals, reptiles, and wild birds. A voice said to him, "Get up, Peter; kill and eat!"

But Peter said, "Certainly not, Lord! I have never eaten anything ritually unclean or defiled."

The voice spoke to him again, "Do not consider anything unclean that God has declared clean." This happened three times, and then the thing was taken back up into heaven.

Acts 10:1–5, 9–16 (GNT)

# Peter Receives an Invitation

## Acts 10

MEANWHILE, AS PETER WAS PUZZLING over the vision, the Holy Spirit said to him, "Three men have come looking for you. Get up, go downstairs, and go with them without hesitation. Don't worry, for I have sent them."

So Peter went down and said, "I'm the man you are looking for. Why have you come?"

They said, "We were sent by Cornelius, a Roman officer. He is a devout and God-fearing man, well respected by all the Jews. A holy angel instructed him to summon you to his house so that he can hear your message." So Peter invited the men to stay for the night. The next day he went with them, accompanied by some of the brothers from Joppa.

Acts 10:19–23 (NLT)

# Peter Visits the Home of Cornelius

## Acts 10

AS PETER ENTERED THE HOUSE, Cornelius met him and fell at his feet in reverence. But Peter made him get up. "Stand up," he said, "I am only a man myself."

While talking with him, Peter went inside and found a large gathering of people. He said to them: "You are well aware that it is against our law for a Jew to associate with or visit a Gentile. But God has shown me that I should not call anyone impure or unclean. So when I was sent for, I came without raising any objection. May I ask why you sent for me?"

Cornelius answered: "Three days ago I was in my house praying at this hour, at three in the afternoon. Suddenly a man in shining clothes stood before me and said, 'Cornelius, God has heard your prayer and remembered your gifts to the poor. Send to Joppa for Simon who is called Peter. He is a guest in the home of Simon the tanner, who lives by the sea.'"

Then Peter began to speak: "I now realize how true it is that God does not show favoritism but accepts from every nation the one who fears him and does what is right. You know the message God sent to the people of Israel, announcing the good news of peace through Jesus Christ, who is Lord of all.

"He commanded us to preach to the people and to testify that he is the one whom God appointed as judge of the living and the dead. All the prophets testify about him that everyone who believes in him receives forgiveness of sins through his name."

While Peter was still speaking these words, the Holy Spirit came on all who heard the message. The circumcised believers who had come with Peter were astonished that the gift of the Holy Spirit had been poured out even on Gentiles.

Acts 10:25–32, 34–36, 42–45 (NIV)

# A Miraculous Prison Escape

## Acts 12

ABOUT THAT TIME KING HEROD AGRIPPA began to persecute some believers in the church. He had the apostle James (John's brother) killed with a sword. When Herod saw how much this pleased the Jewish people, he also arrested Peter. (This took place during the Passover celebration.) Then he imprisoned him, placing him under the guard of four squads of four soldiers each. Herod intended to bring Peter out for public trial after the Passover. But while Peter was in prison, the church prayed very earnestly for him.

The night before Peter was to be placed on trial, he was asleep, fastened with two chains between two soldiers. Others stood guard at the prison gate. Suddenly, there was a bright light in the cell, and an angel of the Lord stood before Peter. The angel struck him on the side to awaken him and said, "Quick! Get up!" And the chains fell off his wrists. Then the angel told him, "Get dressed and put on your sandals." And he did. "Now put on your coat and follow me," the angel ordered.

So Peter left the cell, following the angel. But all the time he thought it was a vision. He didn't realize it was actually happening. They passed the first and second guard posts and came to the iron gate leading to the city, and this opened for them all by itself. So they passed through and started walking down the street, and then the angel suddenly left him.

Peter finally came to his senses. "It's really true!" he said. "The Lord has sent his angel and saved me from Herod and from what the Jewish leaders had planned to do to me!"

Acts 12:1–11 (NLT)

# Paul and Barnabas Opposed

## Acts 13

AMONG THE PROPHETS AND TEACHERS of the church at Antioch of Syria were Barnabas, Simeon (called "the black man"), Lucius (from Cyrene), Manaen (the childhood companion of King Herod Antipas), and Saul. One day as these men were worshiping the Lord and fasting, the Holy Spirit said, "Appoint Barnabas and Saul for the special work to which I have called them."

### PAUL'S FIRST MISSIONARY JOURNEY

So Barnabas and Saul were sent out by the Holy Spirit. They went down to the seaport of Seleucia and then sailed for the island of Cyprus. There, in the town of Salamis, they went to the Jewish synagogues and preached the word of God. John Mark went with them as their assistant.

Afterward they traveled from town to town across the entire island until finally they reached Paphos, where they met a Jewish sorcerer, a false prophet named Bar-Jesus.

But Elymas, the sorcerer (as his name means in Greek), interfered and urged the governor to pay no attention to what Barnabas and Saul said. He was trying to keep the governor from believing.

Saul, also known as Paul, was filled with the Holy Spirit, and he looked the sorcerer in the eye. Then he said, "You son of the devil, full of every sort of deceit and fraud, and enemy of all that is good! Will you never stop perverting the true ways of the Lord? Watch now, for the Lord has laid his hand of punishment upon you, and you will be struck blind. You will not see the sunlight for some time." Instantly mist and darkness came over the man's eyes, and he began groping around begging for someone to take his hand and lead him.

When the governor saw what had happened, he became a believer, for he was astonished at the teaching about the Lord.

Acts 13:1–2, 4–6, 8–12 (NLT)

# Paul and Barnabas Mistaken for Gods

## Acts 14

WHILE THEY WERE AT LYSTRA, Paul and Barnabas came upon a man with crippled feet. He had been that way from birth, so he had never walked. He was sitting and listening as Paul preached. Looking straight at him, Paul realized he had faith to be healed. So Paul called to him in a loud voice, "Stand up!" And the man jumped to his feet and started walking.

When the crowd saw what Paul had done, they shouted in their local dialect, "These men are gods in human form!" They decided that Barnabas was the Greek god Zeus and that Paul was Hermes, since he was the chief speaker. Now the temple of Zeus was located just outside the town. So the priest of the temple and the crowd brought bulls and wreaths of flowers to the town gates, and they prepared to offer sacrifices to the apostles.

But when the apostles Barnabas and Paul heard what was happening, they tore their clothing in dismay and ran out among the people, shouting, "Friends, why are you doing this? We are merely human beings—just like you! We have come to bring you the Good News that you should turn from these worthless things and turn to the living God, who made heaven and earth, the sea, and everything in them. In the past he permitted all the nations to go their own ways, but he never left them without evidence of himself and his goodness. For instance, he sends you rain and good crops and gives you food and joyful hearts." But even with these words, Paul and Barnabas could scarcely restrain the people from sacrificing to them.

Acts 14:8–18 (NLT)

# Paul Asked for Help in a Vision

## Acts 16

NEXT PAUL AND SILAS TRAVELED through the area of Phrygia and Galatia, because the Holy Spirit had prevented them from preaching the word in the province of Asia at that time. Then coming to the borders of Mysia, they headed north for the province of Bithynia, but again the Spirit of Jesus did not allow them to go there. So instead, they went on through Mysia to the seaport of Troas.

That night Paul had a vision: A man from Macedonia in northern Greece was standing there, pleading with him, "Come over to Macedonia and help us!" So we decided to leave for Macedonia at once, having concluded that God was calling us to preach the Good News there.

Acts 16:6–10 (NLT)

CLEVELAND
WOODWARD

# Lydia Becomes a Christian

## Acts 16

[PAUL AND SILAS] BOARDED A BOAT AT TROAS and sailed straight across to the island of Samothrace, and the next day we landed at Neapolis. From there we reached Philippi, a major city of that district of Macedonia and a Roman colony. And we stayed there several days.

On the Sabbath we went a little way outside the city to a riverbank, where we thought people would be meeting for prayer, and we sat down to speak with some women who had gathered there. One of them was Lydia from Thyatira, a merchant of expensive purple cloth, who worshiped God. As she listened to us, the Lord opened her heart, and she accepted what Paul was saying. She and her household were baptized, and she asked us to be her guests. "If you agree that I am a true believer in the Lord," she said, "come and stay at my home." And she urged us until we agreed.

Acts 16:11–15 (NLT)

# Paul and Silas in Prison

## Acts 16

ONE DAY AS [PAUL AND OTHERS] were going to the place to pray, we met a servant-girl who could tell what was going to happen in the future by a demon she had. Her owner made much money from her power. She followed Paul and us crying out, "These are servants of the Highest God. They are telling you how to be saved from the punishment of sin." Paul was troubled. Then he turned and said to the demon in her, "In the name of Jesus Christ, I speak to you. Come out of her!" At once it left her.

The girl's owners saw that they could not make money with her anymore. Then they took hold of Paul and Silas and dragged them to the leaders.

Many people had gathered around Paul and Silas. They were calling out things against them. The leaders had the clothes of Paul and Silas taken off and had them beaten with sticks. After they had hit them many times, they put Paul and Silas in prison. The soldiers told the man who watched the prison to be sure to keep them from getting away. Because of this, they were put in the inside room of the prison and their feet were put in pieces of wood that held them.

About midnight Paul and Silas were praying and singing songs of thanks to God. The other men in prison were listening to them. All at once the earth started to shake. The stones under the prison shook and the doors opened. The chains fell off from everyone.

The man who watched the prison woke up. He saw the prison doors wide open and thought the men in prison had gotten away. At once he pulled out his sword to kill himself. But Paul called to him, "Do not hurt yourself. We are all here!" The man who watched the prison called for a light. Then he ran in and got down in front of Paul and Silas. He was shaking with fear. As he took them outside, he said, "Sirs, what must I do to be saved?"

They said, "Put your trust in the Lord Jesus Christ and you and your family will be saved from the punishment of sin."

Acts 16:16–19, 22–31 (NLV)

# People Turn from Sorcery

## Acts 19

GOD GAVE PAUL THE POWER to perform unusual miracles. When handkerchiefs or aprons that had merely touched his skin were placed on sick people, they were healed of their diseases, and evil spirits were expelled.

A group of Jews was traveling from town to town casting out evil spirits. They tried to use the name of the Lord Jesus in their incantation, saying, "I command you in the name of Jesus, whom Paul preaches, to come out!" Seven sons of Sceva, a leading priest, were doing this. But one time when they tried it, the evil spirit replied, "I know Jesus, and I know Paul, but who are you?" Then the man with the evil spirit leaped on them, overpowered them, and attacked them with such violence that they fled from the house, naked and battered.

The story of what happened spread quickly all through Ephesus, to Jews and Greeks alike. A solemn fear descended on the city, and the name of the Lord Jesus was greatly honored. Many who became believers confessed their sinful practices. A number of them who had been practicing sorcery brought their incantation books and burned them at a public bonfire. The value of the books was several million dollars. So the message about the Lord spread widely and had a powerful effect.

Acts 19:11–20 (NLT)

# A Riot in Ephesus

## Acts 19

A CERTAIN SILVERSMITH NAMED DEMETRIUS made silver models of the temple of the goddess Artemis, and his business brought a great deal of profit to the workers. So he called them all together with others whose work was like theirs and said to them, "Men, you know that our prosperity comes from this work. Now, you can see and hear for yourselves what this fellow Paul is doing. He says that hand-made gods are not gods at all, and he has succeeded in convincing many people, both here in Ephesus and in nearly the whole province of Asia. There is the danger, then, that this business of ours will get a bad name. Not only that, but there is also the danger that the temple of the great goddess Artemis will come to mean nothing and that her greatness will be destroyed—the goddess worshiped by everyone in Asia and in all the world!"

As the crowd heard these words, they became furious and started shouting, "Great is Artemis of Ephesus!" The uproar spread throughout the whole city. The mob grabbed Gaius and Aristarchus, two Macedonians who were traveling with Paul, and rushed with them to the theater.

Meanwhile the whole meeting was in an uproar: some people were shouting one thing, others were shouting something else, because most of them did not even know why they had come together.

At last the city clerk was able to calm the crowd. "Fellow Ephesians!" he said. "Everyone knows that the city of Ephesus is the keeper of the temple of the great Artemis and of the sacred stone that fell down from heaven. Nobody can deny these things. So then, you must calm down and not do anything reckless.

"If Demetrius and his workers have an accusation against anyone, we have the authorities and the regular days for court; charges can be made there."

After saying this, he dismissed the meeting.

Acts 19:24–29, 32, 35–36, 38, 41 (GNT)

# Paul Arrested in Jerusalem

## Acts 21

WHEN WE GOT TO JERUSALEM, the Christians were glad to see us.

The seven days were almost finished. Jews from the countries of Asia saw Paul in the house of God. They made the people turn against him. Then they took hold of him. They cried out, "You who are Jews, help us! This is the man who is teaching against our people and our Law and this house of God. Also he has brought Greek people into the house of God. This has made this holy place unclean." They had seen him before in the city with Trophimus who was from the city of Ephesus. They thought Paul had brought him into the house of God also.

All the people in the city were crying out with loud voices. The people pushed and moved together. They took Paul and dragged him out of the house of God. Then the doors were shut. They were getting ready to kill him. The captain of the soldiers heard there was trouble over all Jerusalem. At once the captain called his soldiers and they ran down to the people. When the people saw the captain and his soldiers, they stopped beating Paul.

### PAUL IS TIED WITH CHAINS

The captain came and took hold of Paul. He told his soldiers to tie Paul with two chains. Then he asked who he was and what he had done. Some of the people called out one thing and some another. The captain was not able to find out what had happened. He told his men to take Paul into the soldiers' building.

Act 21:17, 27–34 (NLV)

# Paul Nearly Beaten

## Acts 22

THE COMMANDER BROUGHT PAUL INSIDE and ordered him lashed with whips to make him confess his crime. He wanted to find out why the crowd had become so furious. When they tied Paul down to lash him, Paul said to the officer standing there, "Is it legal for you to whip a Roman citizen who hasn't even been tried?"

When the officer heard this, he went to the commander and asked, "What are you doing? This man is a Roman citizen!"

So the commander went over and asked Paul, "Tell me, are you a Roman citizen?"

"Yes, I certainly am," Paul replied.

"I am, too," the commander muttered, "and it cost me plenty!"

Paul answered, "But I am a citizen by birth!"

The soldiers who were about to interrogate Paul quickly withdrew when they heard he was a Roman citizen, and the commander was frightened because he had ordered him bound and whipped.

Acts 22:24–29 (NLT)

# A Secret Plot Revealed

## Acts 23

THE NEXT MORNING a group of Jews got together and bound themselves with an oath not to eat or drink until they had killed Paul. There were more than forty of them in the conspiracy. They went to the leading priests and elders and told them, "We have bound ourselves with an oath to eat nothing until we have killed Paul. So you and the high council should ask the commander to bring Paul back to the council again. Pretend you want to examine his case more fully. We will kill him on the way."

But Paul's nephew—his sister's son—heard of their plan and went to the fortress and told Paul. Paul called for one of the Roman officers and said, "Take this young man to the commander. He has something important to tell him."

So the officer did, explaining, "Paul, the prisoner, called me over and asked me to bring this young man to you because he has something to tell you."

The commander took his hand, led him aside, and asked, "What is it you want to tell me?"

Paul's nephew told him, "Some Jews are going to ask you to bring Paul before the high council tomorrow, pretending they want to get some more information. But don't do it! There are more than forty men hiding along the way ready to ambush him. They have vowed not to eat or drink anything until they have killed him. They are ready now, just waiting for your consent."

"Don't let anyone know you told me this," the commander warned the young man.

Acts 23:12–22 (NLT)

# Paul on Trial

## Acts 25 and 26

THREE DAYS AFTER FESTUS ARRIVED in Caesarea to take over his new responsibilities, he left for Jerusalem, where the leading priests and other Jewish leaders met with him and made their accusations against Paul.

About eight or ten days later Festus returned to Caesarea, and on the following day he took his seat in court and ordered that Paul be brought in. When Paul arrived, the Jewish leaders from Jerusalem gathered around and made many serious accusations they couldn't prove.

Paul denied the charges.

"If I have done something worthy of death, I don't refuse to die. But if I am innocent, no one has a right to turn me over to these men to kill me. I appeal to Caesar!"

A few days later King Agrippa arrived with his sister, Bernice, to pay their respects to Festus. During their stay of several days, Festus discussed Paul's case with the king.

So the next day Agrippa and Bernice arrived at the auditorium with great pomp, accompanied by military officers and prominent men of the city. Festus ordered that Paul be brought in.

Then Agrippa said to Paul, "You may speak in your defense."

So Paul, gesturing with his hand, started his defense:

"King Agrippa, do you believe the prophets? I know you do—"

Agrippa interrupted him. "Do you think you can persuade me to become a Christian so quickly?"

Paul replied, "Whether quickly or not, I pray to God that both you and everyone here in this audience might become the same as I am, except for these chains."

Acts 25:1–2, 6–8, 11, 13–14, 23; 26:1, 27–29 (NLT)

# Paul Sets Sail to Italy

## Acts 27

IT WAS DECIDED that [the prisoners] should go to the country of Italy by ship. Then they put Paul and some other men in chains. Julius, a captain of Caesar's army, was to watch them.

The next day we stopped in the city of Sidon. Julius was kind to Paul. He let him visit friends who cared for him.

After leaving Sidon we were blown by the wind along the south side of the island of Cyprus. The wind was against us. The captain found a ship from the city of Alexandria that was going to the country of Italy. He put us on it. For many days the ship did not move fast. It was hard to get to the city of Cnidus. The wind would not let us go on. The wind was against us, and we did not sail very fast. Then we came to a place called Fair Havens. It was near the city of Lasea.

Much time had been lost. To keep going that late in the year would mean danger. Paul spoke with strong words, "Sirs, it looks to me as if this ship and its freight will be lost. We are in danger of being lost also."

The captain of the soldiers listened to what the captain of the ship said and not to what Paul said. It was not a good place to spend the winter. Most of those on the ship wanted to go on and try to get to Phoenix. Crete was a good place to tie up the ship. They wanted to spend the winter there.

Acts 27:1, 3–4, 6–12 (NLV)

# Shipwreck

## Acts 27

ABOUT MIDNIGHT ON THE FOURTEENTH NIGHT of the storm, as we were being driven across the Sea of Adria, the sailors sensed land was near. They dropped a weighted line and found that the water was 120 feet deep. But a little later they measured again and found it was only 90 feet deep. At this rate they were afraid we would soon be driven against the rocks along the shore, so they threw out four anchors from the back of the ship and prayed for daylight.

Then the sailors tried to abandon the ship; they lowered the lifeboat as though they were going to put out anchors from the front of the ship. But Paul said to the commanding officer and the soldiers, "You will all die unless the sailors stay aboard." So the soldiers cut the ropes to the lifeboat and let it drift away.

When morning dawned, they didn't recognize the coastline, but they saw a bay with a beach and wondered if they could get to shore by running the ship aground. So they cut off the anchors and left them in the sea. Then they lowered the rudders, raised the foresail, and headed toward shore. But they hit a shoal and ran the ship aground too soon. The bow of the ship stuck fast, while the stern was repeatedly smashed by the force of the waves and began to break apart.

The soldiers wanted to kill the prisoners to make sure they didn't swim ashore and escape. But the commanding officer wanted to spare Paul, so he didn't let them carry out their plan. Then he ordered all who could swim to jump overboard first and make for land. The others held on to planks or debris from the broken ship. So everyone escaped safely to shore.

Acts 27:27–32, 39–44 (NLT)

# Paul and the Poisonous Snake

## Acts 28

ONCE [PAUL AND THE OTHER PASSENGERS] were safe on shore, we learned that we were on the island of Malta. The people of the island were very kind to us. It was cold and rainy, so they built a fire on the shore to welcome us.

As Paul gathered an armful of sticks and was laying them on the fire, a poisonous snake, driven out by the heat, bit him on the hand. The people of the island saw it hanging from his hand and said to each other, "A murderer, no doubt! Though he escaped the sea, justice will not permit him to live." But Paul shook off the snake into the fire and was unharmed. The people waited for him to swell up or suddenly drop dead. But when they had waited a long time and saw that he wasn't harmed, they changed their minds and decided he was a god.

Near the shore where we landed was an estate belonging to Publius, the chief official of the island. He welcomed us and treated us kindly for three days. As it happened, Publius's father was ill with fever and dysentery. Paul went in and prayed for him, and laying his hands on him, he healed him. Then all the other sick people on the island came and were healed. As a result we were showered with honors, and when the time came to sail, people supplied us with everything we would need for the trip.

Acts 28:1–10 (NLT)

# Paul Witnesses to the Jewish Leaders

## Acts 28

[PAUL AND OTHERS] HAD STAYED ON THE ISLAND three months. Then we left on a ship that had stayed there during the winter.

When we got to Rome, Paul was allowed to live where he wanted to. But a soldier was always by his side to watch him. Three days later Paul asked the leaders of the Jews to come to him. When they had gathered together, he said, "Brothers, I have done nothing against our people or the way our early fathers lived. And yet, I was tied with chains in Jerusalem and handed over to the Romans. I was put on trial, but they found no reason to put me to death. They would have let me go free. But the Jews did not like this. So I had to ask to be sent to Caesar. The reason I have asked you to come is to tell you this. It is because of the hope of the Jewish nation that I am tied in these chains."

They said to Paul, "We have had no letters from Judea about you. No Jew who has come here has ever said anything bad about you. We would like to hear from you what you believe. As for this new religion, all we know is that everyone is talking against it."

Many people came to the place where he stayed. He tried to get them to put their trust in Jesus Christ by preaching from the Law of Moses and from the writings of the early preachers. From morning until night he spoke to them. Some of them believed his teaching. Others did not believe.

Paul paid money to live in a house by himself for two years. He was happy for all who came to see him. He taught about the Lord Jesus Christ without fear. No one stopped him.

Acts 28:11, 16–24, 30–31 (NLV)

# A New Heaven and Earth

## Revelation 1, 21, and 22

THE REVELATION FROM JESUS CHRIST, which God gave him to show his servants what must soon take place. He made it known by sending his angel to his servant John, who testifies to everything he saw—that is, the word of God and the testimony of Jesus Christ.

Then I saw "a new heaven and a new earth," for the first heaven and the first earth had passed away, and there was no longer any sea.

And I heard a loud voice from the throne saying, "Look! God's dwelling place is now among the people, and he will dwell with them. They will be his people, and God himself will be with them and be their God. 'He will wipe every tear from their eyes. There will be no more death' or mourning or crying or pain, for the old order of things has passed away."

And he carried me away in the Spirit to a mountain great and high, and showed me the Holy City, Jerusalem, coming down out of heaven from God. It shone with the glory of God, and its brilliance was like that of a very precious jewel, like a jasper, clear as crystal.

The city does not need the sun or the moon to shine on it, for the glory of God gives it light, and the Lamb is its lamp.

The angel said to me, "These words are trustworthy and true. The Lord, the God who inspires the prophets, sent his angel to show his servants the things that must soon take place."

"Look, I am coming soon! Blessed is the one who keeps the words of the prophecy written in this scroll."

"Look, I am coming soon! My reward is with me, and I will give to each person according to what they have done."

Amen. Come, Lord Jesus.

Revelation 1:1–2; 21:1, 3–4, 10–11, 23; 22:6–7, 12, 20 (NIV)

## A Note to Parents

Welcome to *Kregel's Treasury of Illustrated Bible Stories*! I'm excited to share these wonderful Scriptures and illustrations with you.

While many similar books retell Bible stories, this treasury uses actual Scripture! I have included a variety of translations to render these beloved stories as readable as possible, and have taken great care to present them in context. At times I've condensed stories in order to be able to tell them in short form. Stories have also been placed in a generally agreed upon chronological order, so as to present biblical events within their historical context.

Since nothing can replace the value of reading from your own Bible, I encourage you to explore further in the Word by reading for yourself, and with your children and grandchildren, the complete chapters from which the stories are taken. Starting this practice with your children at a young age can help them establish the important habit of regular Bible reading.

I pray this book is a blessing to you and your children for years to come!

Matt

Matt Lockhart, General Editor

## About the Artwork

The illustrations featured throughout this volume come from one of the largest privately held collections of vintage Bible art. The collection was originally compiled by Standard Publishing, beginning in the early 1900s and continuing for more than fifty years.

Within the collection, there is artwork attributed to over fifty different artists. Of the two hundred fifty works shown in this book, the majority are credited to twenty-four artists. Two American artists noted here together account for more than one hundred of the paintings shown.

**Otto Stemler** (1872–1953): Born in Cincinnati, Ohio, Otto studied at the Cincinnati Art Academy and was Standard's primary in-house artist. Sensitive to how art was reproduced in print, his works often feature bold colors.

**Cleveland Woodward** (1900–1985): Born in Glendale, Ohio, and a graduate of the Cincinnati Art Academy, Cleveland continued his training at the British Academy of Art in Rome. Known for his Bible illustrations, he also spent time in the Holy Land, studying the landscape and traditional attire.

**Matt Lockhart** has been a part of bringing wonderful Bible-based books and resources to life throughout nearly three decades in ministry and Christian publishing. He has a heart for engaging children and adults with the life-giving message of God's Word. He is also the general editor of *Kregel's Easter Treasury of Illustrated Bible Stories* and *Kregel's Christmas Treasury of Illustrated Bible Stories*. Matt and his wife live in Colorado in a nearly empty nest.